COUNTRIES OF THE WORLD

Morocco

Gareth Stevens Publishing
A WORLD ALMANAC EDUCATION GROUP COMPANY

About the Author: William Mark Habeeb is a writer and foreign affairs consultant who has traveled widely throughout North Africa and the Middle East. He holds a Ph.D. in international politics from the Johns Hopkins University.

PICTURE CREDITS

Agence France Presse: 50, 51, 78, 79
ANA Press Agency: 11, 26, 30, 32 (both), 38, 39, 52, 54, 55, 58, 59, 91
Art Directors/TRIP Photo Library: 16, 19, 20, 21, 34, 42, 47, 69, 90 (both)
Michelle Burgess: 19 (top), 30 (top), 62, 64, 68, 81, 82
Christine Osborne Pictures: 7, 8, 18, 25, 28, 33, 43, 56, 57, 65, 66, 72, 80, 87
Focus Team Photo Agency & Press: 63
Getty Images/Hulton Archive: 13, 37, 44, 45, 60, 75, 76, 77
Haga Library Inc.: Cover, 35, 40, 89
HBL Network Photo Agency; 5, 17, 22, 31, 67
Dave G. Houser/Houserstock Inc: 53
I-Africa: 41
International Photobank: 1, 6, 9 (both), 61
John R Jones: 10, 46, 70, 71, 74
Thor Kuniholm/Tangier American Legation Museum: 85
Jason Lauré/Lauré Communications: 27, 29, 73
Lauré Communications: 14, 48
Lonely Planet Images: 23
Sylvia Cordaiy Photo Library: 12
Topham Picturepoint: 15, 36, 49, 84
Nik Wheeler: 4, 24
Amy Zuckerman/Lauré Communications: 83

Digital Scanning by Superskill Graphics Pte Ltd

Written by
WILLIAM MARK HABEEB

Edited by
MELVIN NEO

Edited in the U.S. by
GUS GEDATUS
ALAN WACHTEL

Designed by
GEOSLYN LIM

Picture research by
SUSAN JANE MANUEL

First published in North America in 2003 by
Gareth Stevens Publishing
A World Almanac Education Group Company
330 West Olive Street, Suite 100
Milwaukee, Wisconsin 53212 USA

Please visit our web site at
www.garethstevens.com
For a free color catalog describing
Gareth Stevens Publishing's list of high-quality
books and multimedia programs,
call 1-800-542-2595 (USA) or 1-800-387-3178 (Canada).
Gareth Stevens Publishing's fax: (414) 332-3567.

© **TIMES MEDIA PRIVATE LIMITED 2003**
Originated and designed by
Times Editions
An imprint of Times Media Private Limited
A member of the Times Publishing Group
Times Centre, 1 New Industrial Road
Singapore 536196
http://www.timesone.com.sg/te

Library of Congress Cataloging-in-Publication Data
Habeeb, William Mark.
Morocco / by William Mark Habeeb.
p. cm. — (Countries of the world)
Summary: Discusses the geography, history, government, economy, people, politics, and culture of Morocco.
Includes bibliographical references and index.
ISBN 0-8368-2361-3 (lib. bdg.)
1. Morocco — Juvenile literature. [1. Morocco.] I. Title.
II. Countries of the world.
(Milwaukee, Wis.)
DT305.H24   2003
964 — dc21   2002026856

Printed in Malaysia

1 2 3 4 5 6 7 8 9 07 06 05 04 03

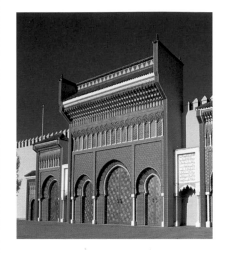

Contents

5 AN OVERVIEW OF MOROCCO

6   Geography
10   History
16   Government and the Economy
20   People and Lifestyle
28   Language and Literature
30   Arts
34   Leisure and Festivals
40   Food

43 A CLOSER LOOK AT MOROCCO

44   Artistic Allure
46   Berbers: The First Moroccans
48   Commander of the Faithful
50   A Desert Challenge
52   Imperial Cities
54   An Islamic Beacon
56   The Jews of Morocco
58   Mint Tea: The National Drink
60   Morocco in the Movies
62   Souq Shopping
64   The Spreading Sands
66   A Struggle for Equality
68   Unique Carpets
70   Volubilis: Ruins of a Roman City
72   Western Sahara: A Disputed Land

**75 RELATIONS WITH
NORTH AMERICA**

For More Information …

86   Full-color map
88   Black-and-white reproducible map
90   Morocco at a Glance
92   Glossary
94   Books, Videos, Web Sites
95   Index

AN OVERVIEW OF MOROCCO

Located in the northwestern corner of Africa, Morocco melds together elements of European, African, and Arabic cultures. While Moroccans are mainly Muslims of Arab descent, the Berbers — Morocco's original inhabitants — maintain their own vibrant community and traditions. The country is also home to one of the Arab world's most significant Jewish communities.

A constitutional monarchy since achieving independence in 1956, Morocco has struggled to reconcile the authority of its kings with its citizens' growing demands for more democratic freedoms. Morocco has entered the twenty-first century with a young population and a new king who is striving to move the nation forward while maintaining its cherished traditions.

Opposite: **Dressed in traditional attire, this Berber girl is adorned with the beautiful silver jewelry that the Berbers specialize in making.**

Below: **The best means of traveling across the deserts of Morocco is on camel. The sure-footed animals can easily make their way across the soft sands.**

THE FLAG OF MOROCCO

Today, Morocco's flag has a red background with a green, five-pointed star in the center. The Moroccan flag that was adopted in the seventeenth century was a solid red banner, similar to the flags of other Arab countries. The five-pointed star, an ancient symbol known as the Seal of Solomon, is believed to have been added by the country's French rulers in 1915 to differentiate the flag. Used on Moroccan coins since the late eighteenth century, the star is believed by Muslims to have magical powers and act as a shield against evil. The star on the flag is green because green is the traditional color of Islam.

Geography

Morocco covers an area of 172,413 square miles (446,550 square kilometers) in the northwestern corner of Africa. The country is bordered on two sides by water: the Mediterranean Sea in the north and the Atlantic Ocean in the west. Located between these two bodies of water is the Strait of Gibraltar, a narrow channel of water that separates Morocco from Europe. Algeria lies to the east and southeast of the country, while the disputed Western Sahara territory, which Morocco has occupied since 1976, is to the south. The Western Sahara, in turn, borders Mauritania and Algeria.

Morocco has a richly varied landscape, and many of the country's major cities, including Casablanca, Tangier, and the capital city of Rabat, are located along the Atlantic coast. The majority of Morocco's population also lives along this relatively narrow coastal strip that features deep-sea ports, small fishing villages, and beautiful, sandy beaches.

IMPERIAL CITIES

Four of Morocco's historic cities — Rabat, Fez, Marrakesh, and Meknes — are known as the "Imperial cities." Each of them has, at one time or another, served as the capital of a Moroccan dynasty.
(*A Closer Look, page 52*)

Below: **Morocco's breathtaking scenery includes deep valleys and rugged mountains.**

Mountains and Deserts

Morocco's most prominent geographic features are the four mountain ranges in the interior of the country and the Sahara Desert in the south and east.

Rising from the Mediterranean coast to a height of 8,058 feet (2,456 meters), the Rif Mountains stretch from the eastern to the western part of the country. The other three mountain ranges, which run in a northeasterly to southwesterly direction, are the Middle Atlas, the High Atlas, and the Anti-Atlas. Jebel Toubkal, Morocco's highest peak, soars 13,665 feet (4,165 m) over the High Atlas range. Morocco's best agricultural land is located in the plains that lie between the mountain ranges and the coast.

The High Atlas and the Anti-Atlas taper off to the south into the barren, inhospitable Sahara Desert. The disputed Western Sahara territory measures 103,000 square miles (266,770 sq km) and is sparsely populated.

Rivers

Most of Morocco's rivers are fed by rain or melting snow in the mountains and drain east into the Sahara Desert or west into the Atlantic Ocean. Among the most important rivers are the Sebou, which runs north of Fez in a valley between the Rif and the Middle Atlas Mountains, and the Oum er-Rbia, which irrigates a fertile valley between the High Atlas Mountains and the Atlantic Ocean.

Above: **Since the land beside the Oum er-Rbia River is fertile, towns are located along its riverbanks.**

THE SPREADING SANDS

The Sahara Desert is the source of a serious environmental problem in Morocco. In recent years, the desert has been slowly expanding, making less and less of the country suitable for habitation.
(A Closer Look, page 64)

Climate

The climate along Morocco's coast is mild and pleasant due to sea breezes. The average daily temperature along the coast is 72° Fahrenheit (22° Celsius) in summer and 57° F (14° C) during winter. The summers are dry, but during autumn and winter, the Mediterranean coast is often cool and wet. The extreme southern Atlantic coast is hot and arid all year round.

The interior of Morocco is warmer. Without the benefit of sea breezes, cities such as Marrakesh are stifling in summer, when the average daily temperature is 80° F (27° C). When hot winds blow in from the Sahara Desert, temperatures can soar above 100° F (38° C). Averaging 53° F (12° C), winter temperatures are cooler but can still be quite warm if the Sahara winds are blowing.

In the mountains, winter temperatures can drop well below freezing, and blinding snowstorms can make travel impossible. Snow often remains on the mountain peaks until well into the spring. Desert areas suffer from intense daytime heat followed by subfreezing evenings. In a single day in Morocco, it is possible to have a snowstorm in the mountains, warm and mild weather on the Atlantic coast, and searing heat in the desert.

Above: **During spring, the Moroccan countryside comes alive with wildflowers.**

Plants and Animals

Morocco's great geographic and climatic diversity is reflected in the country's plant and animal species. Eucalyptus, pine, acacia, and cork oak grow in the forests just inland from the coasts. The argan, a hardy tree found only in Morocco, grows along the lower mountain slopes; pressed argan nut is a source of cooking oil in rural areas. Cedar forests can be found higher up in the mountains. In spring, the mountains are ablaze with wildflowers. The desert's spring-fed oases are home to Morocco's famous date palms.

Mountain gazelles, barbary sheep, and leopards inhabit the higher elevations of the mountains, while macaque monkeys, red foxes, polecats, and lynxes live in the nation's forests. Desert areas are home to a variety of reptiles and insects, as well as gazelles, antelopes, and hyenas.

In spring and autumn, Morocco is host to millions of migratory birds. These bird species include ospreys, storks, herons, flamingos, African marsh owls, and rare bald ibis. Golden eagles live in the mountains, while vultures can be found in the desert regions.

Morocco is also home to a wide variety of sea life. Tuna, swordfish, and mullet inhabit the Mediterranean Sea. Sardines are found along the Atlantic coast, and porpoises and dolphins swim in the Strait of Gibraltar.

Above: **The mountain goat is just one of the many animals that live in the hilly regions of Morocco.**

SOUSS-MASSA NATIONAL PARK

Located along the Atlantic coast near the city of Agadir, the Souss-Massa National Park is a wildlife refuge. The park is the country's most important bird sanctuary.

Left: **These storks are nesting at the top of a dead tree trunk in central Morocco. According to Moroccan tradition, the owners of a house will have good luck if a stork makes its nest on top of the chimney of the house.**

History

Ancient rock paintings discovered in Morocco indicate that the country may have been inhabited as early as 10,000 to 15,000 B.C. During this period, archaeologists believe that the Sahara was made up of forests and grasslands, with abundant wildlife. The Sahara began to turn into the arid desert that it is today only after global climatic changes around 5000 B.C.

The earliest recorded inhabitants of Morocco were most likely the ancestors of today's Berbers. When Phoenician traders first explored the coast of Morocco around 800 B.C., they encountered Berber communities that had established customs, a language, and a livelihood based on agriculture and hunting. Although the Berbers resisted, the Phoenicians succeeded in establishing a number of settlements along Morocco's Mediterranean coast, including what is today Tangier.

By around 400 B.C., the great Phoenician city of Carthage (located in modern-day Tunisia) came to dominate all of North Africa, including Morocco. The Berbers, however, continued to

Below: **The buildings in the Kasbah of Tinerhir are made of earth with palm beam supports.**

resist foreign rule and remained essentially independent in their strongholds in the Atlas Mountain ranges and the Sahara Desert. Carthaginian rule was short-lived. In 146 B.C., the surging Roman Empire conquered Carthage and razed the city to the ground.

Above: **Located in northern Morocco, the ruins of Volubilis are a short distance from the city of Moulay Idriss.**

Roman Morocco

The Romans were content with controlling Morocco's ports and trade routes until around A.D. 50, when they established a number of inland colonies. One colony was Volubilis, a major center of Roman life and culture in Morocco. After Roman agricultural methods were introduced, Morocco became a primary source for the Roman Empire's grain and olive oil.

By A.D. 400, the Roman Empire was in rapid decline. The Vandals seized control of Morocco in A.D. 450, after driving the Romans out of Spain. The Berber tribes continued to maintain their independence in the mountain regions, keeping relentless pressure on the Vandals and later the Byzantines, who tried but failed to reestablish imperial control. For about two hundred years, Morocco was politically unstable and in a state of economic decline.

VOLUBILIS: RUINS OF A ROMAN CITY

Today, Volubilis is in ruins, but the city was once an important outpost of the Roman Empire. It was used as a base from which the Romans ruled the surrounding areas.

(A Closer Look, page 70)

The Islamic Conquest

Arab Muslims invaded North Africa at the beginning of the seventh century, bringing the religion of Islam with them. When the Arab armies reached Morocco at the end of the seventh century, they met with fierce resistance from the Berber tribes. When the Arab conquerors finally gained control of Morocco early in the eighth century, Islam proved an attractive religion to the local population, most of whom converted. The Arab rulers, however, were less welcomed. Although many Arabs settled in Morocco, the Berbers had effectively driven the Arab rulers out of the country by the late eighth century.

Around the same time, Moulay Idriss unified many of the Berber tribes and created the first Moroccan dynasty, with its capital at Fez. The Idrissid dynasty ended in A.D. 828 and was followed by the Almoravid dynasty. With the decline of the Almoravids, the Almohad dynasty rose to prominence in 1160. By 1200, the Almohad empire stretched across North Africa, and Morocco flourished. The Marinids defeated the Almohad empire in 1269, and Morocco came under the rule of their dynasty. The Marinids' rule was shaky, as its rulers were constantly challenged by other families and by rebellious Berber tribes. As Morocco became increasingly weak, European nations began to move in.

CEUTA AND MELILLA

Two cities on Morocco's Mediterranean coast are governed by Spain. Ceuta, a peninsula that juts out into the Mediterranean Sea, has been under Spanish rule since 1580. Melilla (*above*) has been in Spanish hands since 1496. Both of these Spanish-speaking cities house Spanish military bases. The populations of the two cities are primarily of Spanish descent, although Melilla has a sizable Berber community from the nearby Rif Mountains. Melilla has earned a reputation as a center for the smuggling of contraband between Morocco and Europe.

Left: This is an artist's impression of Moroccans guarding their land from foreign invaders in the nineteenth century.

European Intrusion

Portugal established coastal bases in Morocco in the early 1500s, and Spain soon followed. Meanwhile, the Ottoman Empire was approaching from the east, setting the stage for fierce competition over Morocco. A new Moroccan dynasty, the Alaouites, came to power in the 1660s and remains the royal family to this day.

In 1830, France occupied neighboring Algeria. Over the next hundred years, France also expanded its influence and control over Morocco. After making a series of diplomatic deals with its European competitors, France was granted a protectorate over Morocco in 1912, although Spain maintained control over a few coastal outposts.

In 1940, when Nazi Germany invaded and occupied France, the French grip on Morocco weakened. Moroccan nationalists, who wanted Morocco to be an independent state, took the opportunity to set up the Istiqlal, or Independence, Party. After World War II, Moroccan nationalist resistance intensified and received the active support of Sultan Mohammed Ben Youssef, whom the French expelled in 1953. By 1955, the French had relented. Mohammed Ben Youssef made a victorious return from exile, and France began negotiating an end to the protectorate.

Above: **Jubilant Moroccans celebrate the return from exile of Sultan Mohammed Ben Youssef in 1955.**

Independent Morocco

Morocco declared its independence on March 2, 1956. Mohammed Ben Youssef took the name King Mohammed V and declared that he would form a constitutional monarchy. Political instability, however, forced him to take control of the government. In February 1961, the king died suddenly and was succeeded by his son, Hassan II.

Morocco held its first parliamentary elections in 1963. In 1965, however, riots prompted King Hassan II to dissolve parliament and declare a state of emergency. Although new parliamentary elections were allowed in 1977, the king never surrendered his powers. During his rule, Hassan II struggled against opposition groups that called for more democracy and improved human rights. He was also faced with periods of severe economic hardship, which led to riots and labor unrest. Hassan II died in July 1999.

Hassan II was succeeded by his son, Mohammed Ibn Al Hassan, who took the name Mohammed VI. At only thirty-five years of age, Mohammed VI became one of the world's youngest leaders. He promised to reform the Moroccan political system and introduce more freedoms. His early actions in this regard offered hope, and many Moroccans felt an easing of the heavy-handed control that Hassan II had maintained during his reign.

Above: **King Hassan II (*forefront*) makes an appearance at an official function with two of his sons. As the second king of independent Morocco, Hassan II ruled the country from 1961 until his death in 1999.**

14

Moulay Idriss (?–A.D. 791)

Morocco's founder and first king, Moulay Idriss was an Arab who successfully unified many of the country's Berber tribes under his leadership in A.D. 788. The Berbers, who were Muslims, were won over by his religious devotion and his claim of descent from Islam's founder, the prophet Mohammed. Moulay Idriss was so successful in unifying Morocco that an Arab ruler from the east, Caliph Haroun al-Rachid of Baghdad, grew jealous and, in A.D. 791, sent agents to Morocco to poison the Moroccan leader. Moulay Idriss's body was entombed in the town of Moulay Idriss, located near Volubilis. Today, the town is the destination of a yearly pilgrimage. Every August, thousands of people travel to pray and pay homage at Moulay Idriss's tomb.

Moulay Ismail (1645–1727)

Moulay Ismail was the first great king of the Alaouite dynasty. He gained control over all of Morocco, including the rebellious Berber tribes, and he even succeeded in driving the Spanish out of several coastal colonies and the British out of Tangier. Ismail gained so much power that the Ottoman Turks, who occupied neighboring Algeria, dared not invade Morocco. Modeling himself after France's King Louis XIV (r. 1643–1715), who constructed the Palace of Versailles, Moulay Ismail built a complex of palaces in Meknes. Moulay Ismail died in 1727, after ruling Morocco for fifty-five years.

Abd el-Krim (c.1882–1963)

A Berber tribal leader based in the Rif Mountains, Abd el-Krim led an armed rebellion against the Spanish and French, both of whom occupied large parts of Morocco. In 1921, his Berber army defeated a Spanish army, and, in 1925, he launched an attack against French forces. A combined Franco-Spanish effort finally defeated him in 1926. Abd el-Krim was exiled by the French and deported to Reunion, but he managed to escape to Egypt. King Mohammed V awarded him the title of National Hero in 1958. Although Abd el-Krim announced his intention to return to Morocco in 1962, he died before he was able to return to his homeland.

Abd el-Krim

Government and the Economy

Morocco is officially a constitutional monarchy with an elected, multi party legislature. In reality, the king has nearly absolute control over the government, as he appoints the prime minister and approves the cabinet. The king selects the prime minister from the party that holds the majority of seats in the legislature; he may, however, dissolve the legislature at will. As a professed descendent of the prophet Mohammed, the king is a religious authority. He is also both commander-in-chief of the armed forces and the country's foreign policy leader.

The country has a bicameral legislature. The lower house, or Chamber of Representatives, consists of 325 members who are directly elected by the people for five-year terms. Their powers are very limited, although the chamber serves as a forum for the debate and discussion of national issues. The upper house, or Chamber of Counselors, has 270 members who serve

Below: **The Houses of Parliament in the capital city of Rabat are where the Chamber of Counselors and the Chamber of Representatives meet to discuss and debate national issues.**

nine-year terms. They are not elected, but are chosen by various professional associations, labor unions, and local government leaders. The Chamber of Counselors has the power to overturn legislation passed by the Chamber of Representatives.

Throughout his reign, King Hassan II attempted to introduce more democratic elements into the government. He allowed the formation of political parties, including those that opposed his policies. After the 1997 elections for the Chamber of Representatives, the king even chose a former political opponent as prime minister.

Morocco's legal system is based on a combination of Islamic law and civil law adopted from France and Spain. The judiciary is officially independent of the executive and legislative powers, but not of the monarchy. The Supreme Court judges are appointed on the recommendation of the Supreme Council of the Judiciary, over which the king presides.

Local Government

Morocco is divided into sixteen administrative regions that include forty-two provinces and twenty-five prefectures. The prefectures are further divided into *qaidates* (kah-EED-ates), the smallest units of local government. The head of each qaidate is appointed by the Ministry of the Interior.

Above: **The king's palace is located in Rabat, Morocco's capital city.**

COMMANDER OF THE FAITHFUL

Morocco's royal family claims to be descended from the prophet Mohammed. The king is known as the "Commander of the Faithful" and ranks above all other religious authorities in Morocco.

(A Closer Look, page 48)

The Economy

The problems that plague many developing countries — high unemployment, rapid population growth, high government debt, and high rates of poverty — also affect Morocco. The economy is highly dependent on agriculture, which accounts for over 15 percent of the country's income and employs over 40 percent of its workforce. Agricultural exports include citrus fruits, dates, olives, vegetables, and sugar beets. Along the Atlantic coast, the fishing industry employs a substantial portion of the workforce.

Phosphate mining is Morocco's largest industry. Other important industries are leather goods, textiles, and food processing. Many Moroccans are employed in handicrafts, which are widely exported. Tourism is an important industry. Every year, about two million people visit Morocco and spend far more money on food and entertainment than the average Moroccan, thus boosting the economy. Around 35 percent of Morocco's work-force is employed in the services sector, which includes tourism.

About two million Moroccans live and work overseas, mostly in France, Spain, and Belgium. The money that they send home is a vital source of income and helps to alleviate the effects of poverty and unemployment in Morocco.

Above: Since Morocco has one of the world's largest deposits of phosphates, plants such as this one at Khouribga in the northwestern part of the country have been built to process the minerals.

MOROCCO IN THE MOVIES

Morocco's varied natural landscape offers filmmakers the opportunity to shoot in a variety of different climatic regions within one country. This geographic diversity, along with lower production costs, have helped make the country a favored location for Hollywood filmmakers.
(A Closer Look, page 60)

Transportation and Communication

A good road and rail system and an extensive bus network make it convenient for Moroccans to travel around the country. In the congested cities, many people get around on bicycles or motor scooters. Morocco has ten ports that handle commercial ships and passenger ferries. The national airline, Royal Air Maroc, flies to thirty-seven countries, including the United States and Canada.

Morocco's telephone system is ranked among the best in the developing world. Cellular phones are extremely popular and widely used. Internet use has grown rapidly, and Internet cafés can be found in major cities and towns. Many people own satellite dishes that provide access to cable television.

Economic Relations with Europe

Europe is Morocco's largest trading partner and the principal source of foreign investment. In 2000, Morocco and the European Union (EU) signed a free-trade agreement to abolish all trade barriers between them by 2012. The EU also agreed to invest over U.S. $1 billion in the Moroccan economy in the years preceding 2012 to prepare the country for the era of free trade.

Above: Usage of the Internet has grown in Morocco, and many people enjoy web access at Internet cafes such as this one in the city of Zagora.

Below: Casablanca's Mohammed V Airport is one of the major gateways for visitors to Morocco.

People and Lifestyle

Two main ethnic groups, the Berbers and the Arabs, make up Morocco's population of well over thirty million. The Berbers are the country's original inhabitants, and they have maintained their languages and many of their cultural traditions over the centuries. Moroccan Arabs are descendants of Arab invaders who first arrived in Morocco in the seventh century and of Arab Muslims who were persecuted and expelled from Spain in the fifteenth century.

Traditionally, the Berbers have inhabited the nation's mountainous areas, while the Arab Moroccans have lived in its coastal cities. Today, however, many Berbers have migrated to the cities. It is often hard to distinguish between Arab Moroccans and Berbers just by looking at them.

Morocco also has a small population of black Africans descended from slaves who were brought from south of the Sahara Desert and a small Jewish population descended from Jews who fled Catholic Spain. The Western Sahara territory is populated by the Saharawis, a nomadic tribal people who practice herding and subsistence farming.

BERBERS: THE FIRST MOROCCANS

The Berbers have lived in North Africa for a long time, and evidence indicates the presence of Berber culture in Morocco as far back as four thousand years ago.
(A Closer Look, page 46)

Below: These slum areas in Casablanca are the result of overcrowding. Many Moroccan cities lack sufficient housing to accommodate the large number of people that have moved from the countryside to urban areas.

Half of Morocco's population lives in urban areas. Since independence, the country's largest cities have been forced to accommodate millions of migrants from the impoverished rural regions. As a result, slums, poor housing, inadequate health care, and overcrowding plague many Moroccan cities. Due to a high birth rate, Morocco has a young population; 60 percent of the country's people are under the age of twenty-five.

Since it gained independence, Morocco has struggled against poverty, particularly in rural areas. While much progress has been made to increase access to education, health care, and jobs, the country's rapid population growth has made it difficult for the government to ensure economic opportunities for all. Another problem has to do with differences in income; a small segment of the population receives a sizable amount of the country's income, while the majority of Moroccans struggle to make a living. Widespread economic hardship has led to demonstrations and unrest in Morocco's overcrowded cities. Many people earn extra income through the informal economy (sometimes called the "black market"), in which they sell or barter goods and services. Others have turned to illegal activities, and Morocco has become a major supplier of illicit drugs to Europe.

Above: **Morocco has a young population, and many of its younger people have difficulty finding jobs, which increases the country's urban problems.**

WESTERN SAHARA: A DISPUTED LAND

Based on pledges of allegiance made between Saharawi tribes and Moroccan sultans during the eleventh century, Morocco regards the Western Sahara as part of its country.
(A Closer Look, page 72)

Family Life

The family is the most important social unit in Moroccan society, and for the average Moroccan, life revolves around family relationships. Frequently, extended families including grandparents, parents, and children, live in one house. When children marry and have children of their own, a new floor or room may be added to the house to accommodate them. Mealtimes and holidays are major family occasions. Family members are expected to help one another and support other family members who have financial or personal problems. Elderly family members are usually cared for by their children or grandchildren.

In traditional Moroccan society, as in many Middle Eastern cultures, boys are a source of great pride to their parents and are expected to earn a good living and start their own families. Girls are expected to marry — preferably into a good family — and produce grandchildren for their parents. At an early age, girls begin to acquire the skills that will make them attractive to

Above: **In Morocco, many members of a family often live together in one house, making every meal a major occasion.**

potential suitors. Many marriages are arranged, and often the bride and groom do not even meet each other until their wedding day. Moroccan wedding celebrations last for several days and involve both extended families. According to Islamic law, a man may have as many as four wives simultaneously. However, he must first get permission from the existing wives, and he must be able to financially support each wife and her children. As a result, a Moroccan man rarely has more than one wife.

As Morocco becomes more urbanized and increasingly affected by outside influences such as television programs and the Internet, many traditional customs are beginning to change. In cities, for example, young couples often date before marriage, although they still ask their families' permission to marry. Nevertheless, the family unit remains paramount, and young adults who move from rural villages to work in the cities are expected to send money home to help support family members.

Below: After school has ended for the day, this group of boys are on their way to play a game of soccer, one of Morocco's most popular sports.

Education

Literacy is a basic measurement of a country's level of educational development. In Morocco, the literacy rate is quite low, especially among older generations. Only about 44 percent of the total population over the age of fifteen and only about 31 percent of Moroccan women can read and write. This situation is largely the result of years of foreign rule, during which the colonial rulers had no desire to educate the local populations — in urban areas or in rural areas — that did not require literacy to survive.

Since gaining independence, Morocco has struggled to improve its educational system. The government devotes a large portion of the national budget to building schools and hiring teachers and has set a goal of an 80 percent literacy rate by 2010. The challenges Morocco faces in educating its people, however, remain great. The government is unable to keep up with the demand for schools and teachers as a result of rapid population growth and the even more rapid growth of urban areas.

Preschools and kindergartens are concentrated in the cities, but most children do not attend these. The first year of the period

Below: **The government has made education compulsory until the age of thirteen, but a shortage of schools and teachers has resulted in fewer than 70 percent of eligible children attending school; in rural areas attendance is even lower. These Moroccan children attend Khouba el-Bayyadin school in Marrakesh.**

of compulsory "basic education" begins at the age of seven. This period is divided into two cycles. The first cycle lasts for six years and, by law, all children must complete this cycle. The second cycle lasts for three years, and is open to students who have completed the first cycle. Following basic education comes three years of secondary education. During secondary education, students focus either on general studies or on technical education. Students who successfully finish secondary education receive a diploma called a *baccalauréat* (BAH-cah-LOR-ray-ah).

Instruction in the basic and secondary levels is in Arabic, although French is taught from an early age, and many students in secondary schools also study English.

Over 250,000 students are enrolled at Morocco's thirteen universities and fourteen other institutions of higher learning. All courses at university level are taught in French, with the exception of courses in Arabic literature and the Islamic religion. One of the biggest challenges facing Morocco is ensuring employment for its university graduates. Even among those university graduates who secure jobs, many end up employed in jobs that don't require their educational level.

Above: **The language of instruction at Fez University is French, and students who are fluent in the language tend to do better in their studies.**

Religion

Islam is the official religion of Morocco. Over 98 percent of the population is Muslim, and Islamic customs and practices are evident at births, weddings, funerals, and other social events. The country, however, has a small Jewish community and is also home to a number of Christians who are descended from former European colonists.

The Islamic religion was founded in the seventh century in the Arabian Peninsula by Mohammed. Mohammed claimed to have received revelations from God, which he wrote down. These writings became Islam's sacred book, the Qur'an. After Mohammed's death, his followers rapidly spread the new religion throughout the Middle East, North Africa, and into Spain. By the late eighth century, almost all Moroccans had accepted Islam, and Morocco has been an Islamic country ever since.

Like Jews and Christians, Muslims believe in one God, whom they call Allah. They also acknowledge the importance of the Hebrew prophets and Jesus. However, they also believe that

THE FIVE PILLARS OF ISLAM

Muslims follow five guidelines that are known as the Five Pillars of Islam. First, Muslims profess faith in Allah and in Mohammed as his prophet. They also are expected to pray five times a day and give alms to the poor. Every healthy adult Muslim fasts during daylight hours during the holy month of Ramadan. Finally, every Muslim should try to make a hajj, or pilgrimage to the holy city of Mecca.

Mohammed was the final and most important prophet and that the words of the Qur'an are God's ultimate revelation. Muslims observe the Five Pillars of Islam and do not drink alcohol or eat pork. Some strict Muslims also believe that women's faces should be covered by a veil whenever they are in public.

The Muslim place of worship, called a mosque, is the central focus of religious life. Five times a day, a religious official called a muezzin signals that it is prayer time by chanting *Allahu akbar* (ah-LAH-who-AHK-bar) meaning "God is great" through a loudspeaker. On Friday, the Islamic holy day, Muslims prefer to assemble in their local mosques to pray, hear a reading from the Qur'an by a cleric called an imam, and a sermon by another cleric called a *khatib* (kha-TEEB). In small mosques, the same person may hold the position of muezzin, imam, and khatib.

The degree of devotion varies among Moroccan Muslims. Older generations and those living in rural areas are strict in their practices, while younger Moroccans and urban dwellers interpret Islam's rules more loosely. In many Islamic countries, the tension between those who favor a strict interpretation of Islam and those who practice a "modern" version has led to unrest and violence. Morocco has been spared this tension, and everyone is allowed to practice Islam as they wish. The government, however, forbids Muslims to convert from Islam to another religion.

INFLUENCES ON MOROCCAN ISLAM

Most Berbers consider themselves Muslims, but the influence of their traditional customs remains. Throughout the countryside are domed tombs that house the remains of *marabout* (mar-ah-BOOT), or holy men. Every year, thousands of Moroccans, including non-Berbers, make pilgrimages to these tombs. One of the most popular is that of Moulay Idriss, Morocco's first king. Though Islam forbids the worship of saints and holy men, the marabouts' popularity has forced the religious establishment to reluctantly accept them.

THE JEWS OF MOROCCO

Morocco's small Jewish community has survived in the country for over two thousand years.
(*A Closer Look*, page 56)

Left: Although many muezzin today chant through loudspeakers to indicate prayer time, some religious officials, such as this man here, still blow the traditional horn to call devotees for prayer.

Language and Literature

Arabic is the official language of Morocco and the only language used in the country for legal proceedings and other official functions. Arabic is spoken by hundreds of millions of people in North Africa, the Middle East, and the Arabian Peninsula, but the language has many regional dialects that vary from country to country. Written Arabic, however, is the same throughout the world and is revered by Muslims as the language of the Qur'an.

Morocco's distance from the Middle East and its history of close contact with European nations have created a spoken Arabic that incorporates many French words and expressions. Educated Moroccans speak a hybrid dialect using Arabic and French words together in the same sentences.

Three major Berber dialects are still spoken by millions of Moroccan Berbers. Riffian is spoken among inhabitants of the Rif Mountains, Amazigh is used by Berbers in the Middle and High Atlas Mountains, and Tashelhit is spoken by residents of the Anti-Atlas Mountains. These dialects have long oral histories but never developed into written languages. Today, most Berbers speak Arabic. Few non-Berbers speak the Berber dialects.

Left: **Although Arabic is the official language of Morocco, most signs are written in both Arabic and French, reflecting the years when Morocco was under French rule.**

Above: **Newsstands in Morocco tend to stock a mixture of Arabic- and French-language publications.**

French is commonly spoken, and even Moroccans with little schooling are able to converse in basic French. Among well-educated Moroccans and those who engage in international business, French is sometimes preferred over Arabic.

Literature

For centuries, Moroccan literature consisted primarily of poetry and the oral storytelling tradition of the Berbers. A distinctly Moroccan written literature emerged only during the country's struggle for independence in the mid-twentieth century, and much of this writing was political in nature. Even after independence, Moroccan writers focused on political and social themes, and their works were frequently banned by the king. Consequently, several prominent Moroccan writers emigrated to France so they could write more freely about social problems in Morocco.

Fatima Mernissi is a well-known Moroccan feminist author who has been recognized for her book *Beyond the Veil* (1985), which criticizes the treatment of women in Islamic societies. Moroccan authors usually write in French, and only a few have had their works translated into English. As a result, most Moroccan literature is unknown outside Morocco and France.

Arts

Morocco has inspired great artistic creativity among its own people, as well as in artists from abroad who have been captivated by the country's beauty.

Architecture

A unique architectural style has developed in Morocco. This style is most evident in the country's ancient mosques and palaces, the walls and gates that surround its oldest cities, and the magnificent homes of its wealthy citizens. As Islam forbids depictions of human or animal forms, Moroccan architects make intricate geometric designs and shapes in their work, using colorful tiles to adorn interior walls. Passages from the Qur'an, in flowing Arabic calligraphy, are engraved on stone walls. Entrances and doorways are formed in elaborate arches.

Every mosque has a tower, called a minaret, from which the muezzin calls the faithful to pray. While the exteriors of many mosques are plain and austere, the interiors of Morocco's great mosques are stunning. Using tile, wood, and stone, the architects and craftspeople have created spaces that are both serene and grand.

Above: **Koutoubia Mosque is located in the city of Marrakesh. The minarets of all Moroccan mosques are square and not cylindrical, a feature that sets them apart from mosques found elsewhere in the Islamic world.**

AN ISLAMIC BEACON

Ranking among the modern world's grandest religious structures, the Hassan II Mosque (*left*) in Casablanca can hold up to twenty-five thousand people. It has space for another eighty thousand people to gather in the courtyard outside.
(A Closer Look, page 54)

Music and Dance

Morocco's music has been influenced by traditional Berber music, musical styles introduced by the Arabs, and music from southern Spain that was brought over by immigrants.

As the Berbers do not have a written language, music and song have been the principal means of storytelling and recording each tribe's history. The village of Jajouka in the foothills of the Rif Mountains is a center of Berber music. Berber musicians play unique instruments, including various types of drums.

The Arabs who invaded Morocco also brought their musical styles and instruments. The *oud* (OUD) is an instrument similar to the lute, and the *darbuka* (dah-BOO-kah) is a clay drum with a goatskin cover.

Moroccan musical performances are often accompanied by elaborate dances that tell a story or perform a ritual. In rural villages, these dances are performed by men and women together — something that is very rarely seen in the Islamic world, as men and women usually remain segregated.

Above: **Music is an important part of Arab culture in Morocco, and traditional musical instruments are still played by many people today.**

UNIQUE CARPETS

Morocco's rich weaving tradition has created much demand for its carpets and rugs in overseas markets.

(*A Closer Look, page 68*)

SOUQ SHOPPING

The Moroccan *souq* (SOOK) is a traditional shopping area filled with the stalls of hundreds of merchants who sell their goods to both locals and tourists.
(*A Closer Look, page 62*)

Handicrafts and Folk Art

Morocco is world renowned for its handicrafts and folk art. Skilled craftspeople make high-quality products that are mainly sold to people visiting the country.

Moroccan carpets and rugs feature vivid colors and intricate designs. Rugs made by urban weavers can be extremely large, while rural and Berber weavers make smaller rugs. Each Berber tribe incorporates unique designs and colors into its rugs.

Moroccan leather is of a very high quality. The tanneries of Fez have been producing leather, mostly from goatskin, for centuries. Pottery and ceramics are other traditional Moroccan handicrafts, and each region produces its own unique style.

Traditionally, Moroccan Jews make the country's most exquisite jewelry, and many of their masterpieces can be seen in museums. Berbers also make dazzling and elaborately designed jewelry, usually preferring silver to gold. One of the traditional designs produced in Morocco is the Hand of Fatima. Fatima was one of Mohammed's daughters, and jewelry depicting her open hand is thought to bring good fortune.

Below: The Hand of Fatima is a traditional symbol that is used in Moroccan jewelry design because it is believed to bring good luck.

Painters

Because Islam prohibits depictions of humans and animals, many Moroccan artists specialized in arts other than painting. Foreign painters, however, have long been drawn to the natural beauty of Morocco's landscape. In the 1960s, Moroccan painters experimented with abstract art, focusing on geometric shapes, symbols, and the use of color. These artists find inspiration in the country's landscape, as well as in Berber and Arab designs.

Museums

Morocco has dozens of fascinating museums. Many are small archaeological museums tucked away in narrow side streets. Some of Morocco's ancient palaces and houses have been converted into museums that showcase priceless collections of traditional art. Of the larger public museums, the Archaeology Museum in Rabat displays ancient artifacts dating back to the Stone Age, as well as many statues and other remains from the Roman era. Dar Batha Museum in Fez features historical artifacts, tribal carpets, and ceramics. The Museum of Contemporary Art in Tangier houses works by modern Moroccan artists.

ARTISTIC ALLURE

Morocco has been and remains an exciting draw for foreign artists who are inspired by the country's natural beauty.
(A Closer Look, page 44)

Below: **The Museum of Arts and Crafts in Tetouan is a showcase for handicrafts used in daily life in Morocco.**

Leisure and Festivals

Traditionally, Moroccans spend their leisure time with their extended families, visiting one another's homes for meals, and celebrating important family milestones. Families may go on outings, such as trips to the beach or to a city park. Friends meet at neighborhood cafés for coffee, tea, and long conversations. While the family remains the center of social life in Morocco, more and more people in the cities, especially the younger generations, are seeking other forms of entertainment. In Moroccan culture, single men are freer to pursue entertainment outside the home than women. The cafés are filled mostly by men, as are the movie theaters, bars, and discos. Unmarried women are more likely to pursue leisure activities within the family.

In rural and farming areas, leisure is a rare pleasure as most people are preoccupied with earning a living. Weddings and other family celebrations, as well as religious holidays, however,

A STRUGGLE FOR EQUALITY

As in many Islamic societies today, the women in Morocco face a conflict between their cultural traditions and the influences of the modern world.
(*A Closer Look*, page 66)

Below: Women in Morocco tend to spend their leisure time with family and friends. Although they may have traditional values, some Moroccan women dress in Western clothing.

are celebrated as major events. Celebrations in many rural villages may be enlivened by performances by local musicians and dancers. In Berber areas, ancient traditions of storytelling, poetry reciting, and music have survived as forms of entertainment.

Moroccan children take part in all family celebrations and activities. Being part of a close extended family means that the children usually spend a great deal of time with their grandparents, cousins, aunts, and uncles. In large families, there is frequently a family member who is hosting a meal or celebration.

Even at a young age, girls tend to spend time learning to cook, sew, and take care of the house. Boys, however, have more freedom, and their favorite pastime is soccer. Any patch of ground, even a narrow city street, can serve as a makeshift soccer field. Increasingly, Moroccan children are being exposed to television, videos, and other forms of entertainment that are familiar to children in the United States, Europe, and Canada.

Above: **In Morocco, people tend to spend a lot of time with their friends and families. When not visiting one another at home, they also like to meet in cafés to chat.**

Sports

Moroccans are crazy about soccer, and for good reason: Morocco's national soccer team — nicknamed the Lions of the Atlas — has been consistently ranked as one of the best in Africa. In 1970, Morocco's national team became the first African team to qualify for the final rounds of the World Cup Competition. In the 1986 World Cup, Morocco advanced to the round of sixteen finalists, becoming the first African or Arab team to ever do so, before losing to Germany. The Lions of the Atlas play many of their international matches in Casablanca's Mohammed V Stadium, which seats over eighty thousand people.

As King Hassan II was an avid golfer, he promoted the construction of golf courses throughout the country. He also inaugurated several international golf tournaments, and the annual Moroccan Open, played in Rabat, has become a major event on the international golf circuit. Golf tours to Morocco have become an important part of the tourism industry.

A DESERT CHALLENGE

The Marathon of the Sands is a grueling foot race that takes place in the Sahara Desert over a period of seven days.
(*A Closer Look, page 50*)

Below: **On May 27, 1998, the Moroccan national soccer team played against England in the King Hassan II International Cup. Moroccan goalkeeper Driss Benzakri (*right*) and a team member look on as Michael Owen (*left*) of England scores.**

Morocco has produced some extraordinary world-class athletes. Hicham al-Guerrouj, the country's most famous international athlete, holds the world record for the one-mile (1.6-km) run, which he set in 1999. He also holds the world record for the 1,500-meter run. Nawal al-Moutawakil became the first woman from an Arab country to win an Olympic Gold Medal in the 400-meter hurdles race at the 1984 Los Angeles Olympics. In the 2000 Sydney Olympics, Moroccans won four medals for track- and-field events and one medal for boxing.

Festivals and Holidays

In addition to important family celebrations, such as weddings, Moroccans celebrate many religious and cultural festivals throughout the year. The biggest Islamic festival is the month of Ramadan, during which Muslims refrain from eating or drinking during daylight hours. As a result, the pace of life slows, and offices and schools may close early. Each evening, as soon as the sun sets, families and friends gather for a meal called *iftar* (if-TAR), or breaking of the fast. This is a time of togetherness and prayer. The end of Ramadan is celebrated by a holiday called *Eid al-fitr* (ead al-FIT-er), which lasts for four or five days. Routine life comes to a halt during the Eid al-fitr, as families visit relatives and friends and take turns hosting elaborate meals.

Another important religious holiday is *Eid al-adha* (ead al-AD-hah), or feast of the sacrifice. This three-day holiday commemorates the Old Testament story of Abraham, who was willing to sacrifice his son Isaac on God's command. On this holiday, families in rural areas ritualistically slaughter a sheep or lamb. In urban areas, however, people often just eat a symbolic meal of roast lamb.

Moroccans also celebrate other religious feasts and holidays, such as the Islamic New Year and Mohammed's birthday. Islamic holidays do not occur on the same date every year because the Islamic calendar is based on the lunar cycle, in which each month begins with the sighting of the new moon.

The Berbers hold festivals in honor of local holy men. These festivals blend religious rituals and tribal culture. They include not only prayer services but also music and dancing. One of the grandest festivals honors Moulay Idriss. Even the king attends this event held in the village of Moulay Idriss, where the tomb of Morocco's first king is located.

One of Morocco's most interesting festivals occurs in the village of Imilchil, located in the Middle Atlas Mountains. Every year, thousands of people gather for a three-day long marriage festival in which young women choose their husbands. The event is colorful and lively, with music and dancing, and it is attended by hundreds of potential brides and grooms.

Below: **The Imilchil Marriage Festival is a three-day event during which women, including those who are divorced or widowed, can find husbands.**

Food

One of the world's great cuisines, Moroccan food combines traditional Berber dishes with spices from the Arab world and ingredients from Spain. Spices in a traditional Moroccan kitchen include cinnamon, cardamom, saffron, nutmeg, cumin, and hot peppers, along with fresh olive oil, vegetables, and lemon and orange peel. The main staple food of the Moroccan diet is couscous, a grain made of cracked wheat. Moroccan meals often center on vegetables, but meats such as chicken, pigeon, or lamb are also served. For holidays and major feasts, a whole lamb may be roasted over charcoal. Along the coasts, seafood is popular and readily available fresh from the day's catch.

A typical Moroccan meal begins with appetizers, including soups and salads made of shredded carrots, eggplant, or beets, served with hot, flat bread that is used to scoop up the salads. The main course may be a couscous dish in which a mound of steaming couscous is topped with cooked vegetables or meat. A popular dish is *tagine* (tah-JEEN), a stew of spiced vegetables and meat. One of the most tasty Moroccan dishes is *pastilla* (pas-TIL-lah), a delicate pastry stuffed with pigeon meat, eggs, cinnamon, and sugar. Virtually every Moroccan dish is served with *harissa* (hah-REE-sah), a sauce made from hot peppers, olive

Left: **A dish popular with many Moroccans is tagine, a stew of spiced vegetables and meat.**

Above: **People living in the cities will often stop for a quick meal at outdoor stalls selling dishes such as roast chicken or lamb kabobs.**

oil, and garlic. The sauce can be extremely hot, and diners are free to add as much or as little as they wish.

For dessert, Moroccans eat pastries stuffed with almond paste or plates of fresh fruit and nuts. Every meal ends with mint tea, Morocco's national drink. Coffee is widely available and is sometimes spiced with cardamom or cinnamon. Moroccan children, like children everywhere, drink soft drinks and fruit juice. Every city has small shops or street vendors selling freshly squeezed orange, watermelon, or grape juice.

For a quick meal in the city, Moroccans stop by a food stall serving roast chicken with French fries or lamb kabobs — small pieces of lamb and vegetables on skewers. *Kafta* (KAHF-tah), or ground lamb, is served with chopped tomatoes and a hot sauce in rolled up flat bread — the Moroccan version of a hamburger!

Morocco's major cities have restaurants serving Moroccan or French cuisine that cater principally to tourists and wealthy Moroccans. Most Moroccans eat their meals at home, with the exception of snacks or quick meals bought from street stalls. In villages and rural areas, restaurants are rare, although even the smallest town will have a café that serves snacks.

MINT TEA: THE NATIONAL DRINK

Mint tea was introduced to Morocco by British merchants in the middle of the nineteenth century, and it has become the country's national drink.
(A Closer Look, page 58)

A CLOSER LOOK AT MOROCCO

Morocco's rich culture and society have been shaped and influenced by many peoples, including the Berbers, the country's original inhabitants; foreign conquerors from Rome, the Arab world, and Europe; and Jewish immigrants fleeing fifteenth-century Spain. The result is a unique Moroccan identity that has contributed to the world in the areas of architecture, music, the arts, and politics.

Opposite: **Moroccans have a strong musical tradition and even young children are taught to play musical instruments.**

While Morocco is an ancient society, the country is young. Independent for less than fifty years, Moroccans today are struggling with many conflicts and tensions that confront their changing

society. Despite being a breathtakingly beautiful country, Morocco is threatened by serious environmental challenges, and its leaders must ensure that the nation's youthful and growing population is employed. Although Morocco remains a devout Islamic nation, young Moroccans are attracted by Europe and the West, which are less strict about public behavior. Young Moroccan women, in particular, seek opportunities that were not available to their mothers.

Above: **In the Atlas Mountains, farmers still harvest wheat using horses.**

Despite these challenges — or perhaps because of them — Morocco is a dynamic and fascinating nation that is proud of its monumental past and committed to its promising future.

Artistic Allure

As a result of European colonial expansion into North Africa and the Middle East in the nineteenth century, European artists were able to travel to the deserts, small villages, and exotic cities of the Islamic world. Many artists developed a deep fascination with what they called "the Orient." They were attracted not only to the people but to the incredible landscapes and vistas. Morocco, being in close proximity to Europe and increasingly open to the French, quickly became one of the most popular destinations for artists seeking the experience of the Orient.

One of the first artists to travel to Morocco was Ferdinand Victor Eugene Delacroix (1798–1863), a French painter who journeyed there in 1831. Delacroix was overwhelmed by the brilliant, natural colors of Morocco, which were made even more intense by the bright Mediterranean sunlight. He was also fascinated by the people he met: the veiled women, the soldiers in uniform, and the Berbers in traditional clothing. Delacroix filled dozens of notebooks with sketches and watercolors, and, on his return to Paris, he incorporated Moroccan scenes in his works. Delacroix inspired many other French artists to travel to Morocco, and the works they produced became known as "Orientalist painting."

In the 1870s, American artist Louis Comfort Tiffany (1848–1933) visited Morocco. Tiffany is best known for his decorative stained-glass lamps and windows. He credited his sojourn in Morocco as a source of inspiration for his colorful work.

The most famous painter to find inspiration in Morocco was Henri Matisse (1869–1954), who visited the country three times. Matisse found Morocco to be a feast for the senses and was especially attracted to the gardens of Tangier. On his return to France, a Parisian art gallery held a special exhibit of the paintings and sculptures Matisse had made in Morocco. In 1990, a major international art exhibit, entitled *Matisse in Morocco*, traveled to New York, Washington, Moscow, and Leningrad.

As photography developed as a separate art form in the twentieth century, many photographers also were drawn by Morocco's allure. Today, whether through the snapshots of tourists or the photos of professionals, Morocco is without doubt one of the most photographed countries in the world.

Above: **French artist Eugene Delacroix was one of the first foreigners to visit Morocco. Delacroix was fascinated by the country and his works depicted scenes of Moroccan life.**

Opposite: **Regarded as one of the most important French painters of the 20th century, Henri Matisse found inspiration in the beauty of Morocco. He was fascinated by the vibrant colors he saw, leading him to explore and celebrate the use of color in the paintings he produced throughout his career.**

Berbers:
The First Moroccans

The origin of the Berbers is a mystery, but they have lived in North Africa for centuries, and evidence indicates that Berber culture may be four thousand years old. For centuries, the Berbers practiced their own religion, but because they had no written language, very little is known about their customs.

After the Arab-Muslim conquest of Morocco in the seventh century, many Berbers moved to the mountains, where they were able to maintain their traditions, although virtually all Berbers eventually adopted Islam as their religion. The Berbers have a great warrior tradition, and they never completely accepted foreign rule. Most of Morocco's early Arab rulers learned not to challenge the Berbers and left them alone in their mountain strongholds. Two of Morocco's great imperial dynasties — the Almoravids in the eleventh and twelfth centuries and the Almohads in the twelfth and thirteenth centuries — were led by Berbers.

Below: **A Berber man in traditional dress contemplates the Moroccan landscape. The Berbers were traditionally nomadic farmers and shepherds who lived in the mountains. Today, many Berbers have moved to urban areas.**

The mountains of Morocco remain the center of Berber life. Over the centuries, however, many Berbers have moved to Morocco's cities and married people of Arabic descent. Today, over half of all Moroccans have some Berber lineage, making Morocco the world's largest Berber nation. Small communities of Berbers also live in Algeria, Tunisia, and Libya.

While outsiders often speak of the Berbers as a homogeneous group, most Berbers identify themselves first and foremost with their particular tribes. Each tribe speaks its own unique dialect, although none of these are written. Each also has a unique musical and dancing tradition. Original Berber art- and craftwork are among the most beautiful products in Morocco. Various Berber tribes also specialize in producing silver jewelry decorated with unique tribal motifs and designs, carpets, and leather products.

In recent years, Berber organizations in Morocco have protested against what they see as efforts to eradicate their culture. These organizations have complained that only Arabic and French have been granted the status of official languages, even though millions of Moroccans speak Berber dialects. In addition, they have campaigned to have Berber dialects taught in schools to keep them from dying out. Berbers also have sought a greater role in Moroccan politics.

Above: **Although many Berbers have moved to the cities in search of better employment opportunities, some still live in the mountains and teach their children the traditional customs and language of their heritage.**

Commander of the Faithful

Morocco's royal family, the Alaouites, has ruled the country since the middle of the seventeenth century. Even during periods of foreign control, such as when the country was a French protectorate from 1912 to 1956, the Alaouites were widely regarded by Moroccans as their nation's rightful rulers.

The Alaouite family claims to be descended from the prophet Mohammed's daughter, Fatima. While this claim cannot be proved, most Moroccans believe it to be true. As a result, the Alaouites have enjoyed political power and religious authority for the past two hundred and fifty years. The king is known as the "Commander of the Faithful," and ranks above all other religious authorities in Morocco.

In recent years, many governments in the Muslim world have had their power and authority challenged by religious extremists who believe that their governments are illegitimate and should be replaced by Islamic governments. Morocco, however, has been largely immune to this problem because of the widespread acknowledgement, even by the country's religious leaders, of the king's religious authority.

Left: **As Commander of the Faithful, the Moroccan king is the country's highest religious leader. Here, King Hassan II works with an imam.**

Morocco's kings have had great freedom in addressing the country's many social and economic problems. The country has been the scene of riots and protests against various government policies, but Moroccans rarely criticize the royal family. Even leaders who oppose certain policies express loyalty to the king.

The current king, Mohammed VI, began his educational training at the age of four at a religious school in the Royal Palace, where he learned the Qur'an and Islamic law. He later studied law and politics in France. Mohammed VI was not married when he assumed the throne upon the death of his father in 1999. In spring 2002, he married a young computer engineer in a festive wedding ceremony in Fez. She is known as Princess Lalla Salma because Morocco's monarchy has no tradition of queens.

A Desert Challenge

The barren Sahara Desert in southern Morocco is the location of the Marathon of the Sands, which is known as the world's toughest foot race. Competitors cover 145 miles (233 km) across the desert's sandy terrain over a period of seven days, sleeping in tents at night. During the day, they endure scorching temperatures that can reach as high as 120° F (49° C) while running up shifting sand dunes and craggy cliffs. At night, temperatures in the desert can plummet to a chilly 40° F (4° C), and competitors often have to contend with desert snakes and scorpions trying to find their way into the tents. Participants may even have to sit in their tents through sandstorms.

Competitors in the marathon are expected to carry seven days worth of food and other supplies in a backpack. They are only allowed 2.5 gallons (9.5 liters) of water per day. The water is distributed at designated check points along the route.

Below: **Participants in the Marathon of the Sands, which is also called the Marathon des Sables, walk in single file to minimize the impact of the strong desert winds.**

Surprisingly, since 1986, hundreds of runners from around the world have found the Marathon of the Sands to be great fun — or at least a great challenge. This grueling marathon is sponsored annually by the Moroccan Ministry of Tourism and a French sports organization called Atlantide Organisation Internationale. For the privilege of participating in this race, competitors pay U.S. $2,500, while the winner collects U.S. $5,000.

In some years, the event has attracted over five hundred participants, although many drop out well before the finish line. The exact course of the race changes from year to year, and the route is only made known to the competitors on the morning of the race. Despite the race's grueling nature, a festive atmosphere prevails — especially at the finish line, where bands play and crowds cheer as the successful runners come straggling in.

The Marathon of the Sands has attracted considerable attention from the world media, and each year the runners are closely followed by reporters, photographers, and television crews in all-terrain vehicles. The race also has raised greater awareness of the awesome beauty and the immense power of the Sahara.

Above: **The competitors in what has been called the world's toughest foot race have to deal with scorching daytime temperatures, chilly nights, and sand storms, while running on shifting sand dunes for seven days.**

Imperial Cities

Rabat, Fez, Meknes, and Marrakesh are known as the "Imperial cities" because each has served as the capital of a Moroccan dynasty at one time or another.

Fez was established around A.D. 800 by Idriss II. Among its first inhabitants were Muslims who had been forced out of Catholic Spain. These settlers brought with them a rich cultural heritage that, combined with the influence of Arabs from the East and local Berbers, created a vibrant and unique city. Today, the *medina* (ma-DEE-na), or old, walled, center area, of Fez, remains virtually unchanged from medieval times. The Fez medina is made up of over nine thousand narrow streets, alleyways, and passages, and its many souqs are among the most fascinating in Morocco.

In A.D. 1062, the Almoravid dynasty founded the city of Marrakesh to serve as its capital. Sitting at the foot of the Atlas Mountains, Marrakesh is a beautiful city of gardens, palaces, and

Below: **Founded in A.D. 800, the vibrant and colorful city of Fez is among Morocco's oldest cities.**

souqs. As the most southerly of the Imperial cities, Marrakesh has been a crossroads for trade and commerce for centuries.

Meknes, the city that Alaouite king Moulay Ismail made his capital in 1672, lies in the Middle Atlas Mountains. Moulay Ismail ruled at the same time as King Louis XIV of France, and he was determined to make his capital as glorious as the French king's palace at Versailles. He built extensive walls around Meknes, with monumental gates providing entry into the city, and adorned his city with gardens, mosques, and fountains. Work also began on a palace complex, the ruins of which still stand today. Upon Moulay Ismail's death in 1727, the imperial seat was moved to Marrakesh, and much of the planned construction in Meknes remained unfinished.

The coastal city of Rabat briefly served as Morocco's imperial capital in the twelfth century under the Almohad dynasty, but the city's real importance began in 1912, when the French moved their colonial capital to Rabat from Fez. Rabat has been Morocco's capital ever since, and today is the seat of the monarchy and the home of the country's king.

Above: **Moulay Ismail, who founded the city of Meknes, wanted it to be as splendid as the palace at Versailles in France. This series of ancient arches form a walkway that is part of the palace complex.**

An Islamic Beacon

In 1980, Morocco's King Hassan II decided to build a mosque that would rank among the world's grandest religious structures. A site in Casablanca, on the Atlantic coast, was chosen so that the mosque would serve as a beacon of Islam to the world. The mosque was to reflect Morocco's — and the king's — unshakeable commitment to Islam and serve as a showcase of Moroccan craftsmanship and design. Contributions from the citizens raised most of the nearly U.S. $700 million needed to build the mosque.

Work on the mosque began in 1986. Although the architect was French, over thirty thousand Moroccans worked on the project, including ten thousand professional craftspeople and artisans. The mosque formally opened in 1993, just in time to celebrate the king's sixtieth birthday. In just seven years, Moroccans had built one of the world's greatest religious edifices.

The Hassan II Mosque is so immense that it can accommodate twenty-five thousand worshipers inside, while another eighty thousand can congregate in the courtyard outside. The mosque's marble minaret soars as tall as a 50-story building. At night,

Below: **The Hassan II Mosque in Casablanca is the world's largest modern Islamic structure and has a 50-story-high minaret that can be seen for miles around.**

Above: **The interior of the Hassan II Mosque is decorated with exquisite tilework, traditional wood carvings, and decorative molding.**

a laser projects a beam of light from the top of the minaret toward Mecca, Islam's holiest city. The roof of the mosque is retractable so that on clear evenings worshipers can contemplate the infinite stars as they pray. Within the grounds of the complex are a religious school, a library, and a conference center.

Size alone does not convey all that is special about the Hassan II Mosque. Even more impressive is the exquisite Moroccan craftsmanship. Wood carving, tilework, and decorative molding adorn the building. Muslims are required to wash their hands and feet before praying, and the courtyard of the mosque contains dozens of fountains built for this purpose, each one beautifully decorated with mosaic tiles. Peaceful, well-maintained gardens surround the mosque, making it a favorite destination for family outings and a good place to escape from the bustle of Casablanca.

Some Moroccans believe the mosque was too elaborate and too expensive for a country struggling with poverty and other social problems. Virtually everyone who visits it agrees, however, that the mosque represents the traditional craftsmanship and modern talents of the Moroccan people. Most Moroccans today are extremely proud of the Hassan II Mosque.

The Jews of Morocco

Jews have lived in Morocco for over two thousand years, and scholars believe that they may have been in Morocco since 600 B.C. After the Romans destroyed the Israelites' second temple in Jerusalem in A.D. 70, a wave of Jewish refugees spread across North Africa, many of whom settled in Morocco. Even though Islam is tolerant of other religions, many Moroccan Jews were forced to convert to Islam by the Arab Muslims who conquered Morocco. Many Jews continued to practice their religion in secret.

In 1391, the Catholic rulers of Spain persecuted thousands of Jews, causing many of them to flee to Morocco, as the country was still considered a safer place for Jews than Catholic Europe. Life, however, was not perfect for the Jews of Morocco. By the middle 1400s, the Jewish community in Fez had been separated from the city's Muslim population and forced to live in its own quarter, called a *mellah* (MEL-la). Periodically, Jews who refused to convert to Islam suffered from violence at the hands of Muslims.

More positive interaction between Jews and Muslims did take place, contributing to Morocco's cultural diversity and richness. When Spain expelled its entire Jewish community in 1492, the Moroccan sultan welcomed thousands of Jewish immigrants. Over the following centuries, the condition of Morocco's Jewish

Left: **The city of Fez is home to a Jewish cemetery. Jews have lived in Morocco for many years, and they have contributed to the country's culture in many ways.**

Left: These Moroccans are sitting in front of the entrance to the Jewish cemetery in Fez. At its peak, Morocco was home to about 300,000 Jews.

community swung between periods of persecution and prosperity.

When the French established a protectorate over Morocco in 1912, they decreed that the Jews must be treated equally. Many Moroccan Jews learned French and developed business relationships in France. During World War II, when France was defeated by Germany, Sultan Mohammed V of Morocco refused to allow any Moroccan Jews to be deported. The sultan publicly vowed to protect the property and lives of Morocco's Jews.

Many Moroccan Jews chose to emigrate to the state of Israel when it was established in 1948; others went to North America and Europe. The Jewish population in Morocco fell from 300,000 in 1950 to 200,000 at the time of Morocco's independence in 1956. Morocco's new constitution guaranteed the rights of the Jewish community, and both King Mohammed V and King Hassan II have maintained good relations with Jewish leaders. However, growing tension between the Arab world and Israel, as well as limited economic opportunities in Morocco, has caused more Moroccan Jews to leave. Today, fewer than 10,000 Jews live in Morocco, while more than 600,000 Jews of Moroccan descent live in Israel and another 250,000 live in France. Many Moroccan Jews who emigrated have warm feelings toward their ancestral home, and they often visit and extend support to the Jews that remain there.

MOROCCO AND PEACE IN THE MIDDLE EAST

King Hassan II was a strong advocate of peace between the Arab world and Israel and was among the first Arab leaders to meet with Israel's leaders. He frequently invited Moroccan Jews who had emigrated to return for visits. Hassan II was instrumental in arranging Egyptian president Anwar el-Sadat's historic trip to Israel in 1977, and immediately after Israel and the Palestine Liberation Organization (PLO) signed a peace agreement in Washington, D.C., in 1993, Israeli prime minister Yitzhak Rabin flew to Morocco to personally thank King Hassan for his assistance.

Mint Tea:
The National Drink

Tea was introduced to Morocco by British merchants in the middle of the nineteenth century, and it has since become the country's national drink. Moroccans drink a unique form of mint tea throughout the day, and the drink is more popular than coffee or soft drinks. People carrying trays of tea are common sights on the streets and alleys of Moroccan souqs, where shopkeepers offer customers a glass of tea, or sometimes several glasses of tea, before any business is conducted. In even modest homes, a pot of tea will be brought out as soon as guests arrive. Every meal ends with tea.

Moroccans use green tea imported from China. Green tea is more delicate than the black tea drunk by most North Americans and Europeans, and has a light golden color. Tea bags are never used. Rather, the ground green tea leaves are added directly to a pot of boiling water. Next, handfuls of fresh mint leaves are added, followed by lots of sugar. The tea is left to steep for several minutes, and the result is a refreshing and very sweet glass of mint-flavored tea.

Left: **A Moroccan enjoys a refreshing cup of mint tea in one of the nation's many teahouses. In Morocco, mint tea is drunk throughout the day, and it is usually offered to guests before the start of any serious business discussions.**

Moroccans drink tea from small, clear glasses rather than from cups or mugs. These special glasses made just for tea drinking are decorated with painted designs and are among a family's most treasured possessions. Because the glasses have no handles, they get very hot; Moroccans have perfected a way of holding their glasses at the rim with the tips of their fingers.

The person chosen to serve the tea to guests, or after a dinner or banquet, is very honored. The server ceremonially places the tea, mint leaves, and sugar in a large silver teapot, then waits for it to steep. The server drinks the first glass to make sure the balance of tea, mint, and sugar is correct. When the tea is ready, the server pours it from the teapot into the small glasses arranged on a tray. Some tea servers, especially waiters in restaurants, hold the teapot high in the air as they theatrically pour it in a long stream into the glasses. It is customary for people to drink at least two or three glasses of tea.

Above: **There is an art to brewing and drinking mint tea. The server must follow a set routine before pouring the tea into special, small, clear glasses.**

Morocco in the Movies

Morocco's varied natural landscape, its generally warm and sunny climate, and its exotic cities are attractive to filmmakers from around the world. In Morocco, a director can shoot scenes in a desert, a mountain, a forest, a city, or along a coast, all within the span of a few days. The country's diverse regions can be used to represent areas that are difficult or impossible for directors to work in, such as the deserts of Arabia or the snow capped peaks of Tibet. It is less expensive to film a movie in Morocco than in the United States or Europe, and the government has made great efforts to assist foreign filmmakers.

French filmmakers were the first to discover Morocco, and they began producing films there as early as the 1920s. In 1949, American director Orson Welles filmed Shakespeare's *Othello* in Morocco. The Academy Award-winning *Lawrence of Arabia* was shot in the Moroccan Sahara in 1969. Another Academy Award-winning film, *Patton*, starring George C. Scott as the famous U.S. World War II general, was also shot in Morocco.

Below: Hollywood films that have been shot in Morocco include *Black Hawk Down,* the true story of a U.S. military operation in Somalia.

Morocco has often been the location of films about Biblical times and the Holy Land; *Jesus of Nazareth* by Franco Zeffirelli and *The Last Temptation of Christ* by Martin Scorsese are among the most well known. Scorsese returned to Morocco in 1996 to film *Kundun*, the story of the Dalai Lama, using the Moroccan mountains to represent Tibet. In *Jewel of the Nile*, Kathleen Turner, Michael Douglas, and Danny DeVito travel hundreds of miles across North Africa, but the filming actually took place in a relatively small corner of Morocco near the city of Fez. *Black Hawk Down*, the true story of a U.S. military operation in the African nation of Somalia, was another blockbuster shot in Morocco. Ironically, the film that most moviegoers associate with Morocco — *Casablanca*, starring Humphrey Bogart and Ingrid Bergman — was filmed on a Hollywood set. The actors never set foot in Morocco!

Moroccan film companies, many of which have great technical resources, often assist in the filming and production of foreign-made films. The Moroccan film industry is small but has produced some excellent work. Unlike foreign directors, who are attracted by the country's physical diversity, Moroccan directors focus on the country's social structure. Increasingly, Moroccan films are being shown at international film festivals. The government has helped establish several film festivals in Morocco to encourage Moroccan directors to make more films.

Above: **Morocco offers filmmakers the opportunity to shoot in a variety of locations. An example is this village in central Morocco that has been used as a set in several movies, including *Gladiator,* starring Russell Crowe.**

Souq Shopping

Every Moroccan city has a souq where merchants sell their goods to both Moroccans and tourists. In some ways, a souq is like a shopping mall, with hundreds of shops and thousands of goods available in one central location. The souq is an ancient institution and a vibrant center of social and commercial activity. To walk through a souq is to experience daily life in Morocco.

A typical Moroccan souq is located in the central and oldest part of the city, called the medina. A souq is not a single building but a series of small shops and stalls crammed side-by-side along a labyrinth of narrow streets and passages that are usually clustered around a large, central mosque. To a first-time visitor, the souq appears to be a chaotic and noisy place. In reality, however, souqs are laid out according to the products being sold. One street, for example, may have nothing but rug and carpet

Below: **For Moroccans, the souk is often the best place to shop, as the many merchants sell practically everything they need, including leather goods, carpets, herbs and spices, perfume, textiles, and books.**

sellers. Another alley may be home to vendors selling spices and tea. Once visitors learn where each type of merchant is located, they can quite easily figure out how to go about shopping. It is easy, however, to get lost in a souq as none of the streets or passages are marked.

Large souqs often have a long, central section covered by a vaulted ceiling and having large doors at either end that can be closed and locked at the end of the day. Merchants selling valuable products, such as gold and silver jewelry, congregate in this section, so that their shops can be secured at night.

Shopping in a souq is a unique and challenging experience because buyers are expected to bargain for the items they want. Moroccans know this process well and will generally settle on a mutually agreed upon price fairly quickly. For tourists, the process can be confusing. The merchants will be very gracious and offer mint tea or soft drinks as the visitor examines their wares. A price that is many times more than what the merchants will actually accept is proposed, and it is up to the buyer to counter with a lower price. For expensive items, such as large carpets, the bargaining process can take hours before a price is agreed on.

Above: **Merchandise in souks is displayed to appeal. While some stalls specialize in tourist souvenirs, others cater to the locals, selling items such as traditional leather slippers called** *babouche* **(bah-BOOSH).**

The Spreading Sands

The Sahara Desert, which covers much of the southern and western parts of Morocco, and virtually all of the territory of the Western Sahara, is one of the country's most beautiful natural features. Unfortunately, the Sahara is also the source of Morocco's most serious environmental problem: desertification. This term refers to the steady expansion of the desert, a phenomenon that has been occurring for many decades. Over time, the desert consumes more and more arable land, making less and less of the country suitable for habitation. People are forced to move, and plant and animal species become threatened with extinction.

Desertification is in part a natural phenomenon due to changes in global weather patterns, but it is also caused by the overuse of agricultural land in areas bordering the desert. If farmers, for example, allow the soil to deteriorate by planting too many crops or failing to allow fields to lie fallow periodically, or if communities cut down too many trees for firewood, the soil

Below: Desertification is a serious threat in Morocco and the country's government takes several measures to fight it. One tactic is to build palm-frond barriers, such as these, in the desert in order to contain the sand within a specific area.

loses its ability to retain water and sustain life, and the land ultimately becomes barren. When the land becomes barren in regions close to the Sahara, the desert spreads, and the farming community has to move to nearby lands, where desertification can continue. The problem has been aggravated by Morocco's rapid population growth; more people means a greater need for food, which, in turn, leads to an overuse of agricultural land.

Moroccans are aware of the urgency of the problem and are committed to addressing it. The government of Morocco is working with farmers to improve agricultural techniques to minimize soil damage. Irrigation projects are also creating more farmland in areas that are away from the desert. Perhaps the most important way in which Morocco is addressing the problem of desertification is by trying to reduce the country's birth rate, which is among the world's highest; ultimately, desertification, along with urban pollution and other environmental problems, can only be fought successfully by reducing the demand for resources. The Sahara can then return to being a source of beauty and awe rather than a threat to Morocco's future.

Above: **Because strong desert winds blow loose sand particles across the land, specially designed barriers, such as this one, have been constructed to stop sand from blowing onto roads and becoming a hazard to motorists.**

A Struggle For Equality

Moroccan women, like other women in Muslim societies, face a conflict between tradition and modernization. Traditionally, women marry, tend the household, raise children, and submit to their husbands' authority. Modernization, however, has encouraged women to seek education, employment, and greater personal independence. The fact that Moroccans have historically been receptive to foreign influences, yet cherish their traditions, has made this conflict very difficult for many Moroccan women.

Moroccan family law is based on the teachings of the Qur'an. Under the law, women may not marry without the permission of their fathers or guardians, and when they marry, they transfer most rights to their husbands. The law specifically states that the family is under the direction of the husband and that the wife has to obey him. In the event of divorce, the father is usually granted custody of the children. Women are not automatically entitled to financial support and are allowed to inherit only half as much as any male heirs in their families. The result is that many divorced Moroccan women end up living lives of desperation and poverty.

Below: **The literacy rate among Moroccan women is lower compared to that of men. The Moroccan government has attempted to provide more educational opportunities for women by organizing special classes such as this one in Rabat.**

Left: Women in Morocco have made clear progress in the workforce. In 1973, only 8 percent of Moroccan women worked outside the home. Today, the number is around 25 percent.

King Hassan II attempted to implement some limited reforms in Moroccan family law, including increasing the minimum age of marriage from fifteen to eighteen, allowing women to claim half of all joint property in the case of divorce, and allowing divorced mothers who remarry to regain custody of their children. These proposals have drawn fierce opposition from Islamic and traditionalist groups in Morocco, including many religious women. Although pro-reform groups are vocal in supporting the reforms, no progress has been made in implementing them. King Hassan II was more successful in advancing women's political rights. The 1972 constitution granted women the right to vote, and by the early 1990s, several women had been elected to parliament.

In recent years, numerous organizations have been established — some with the government's encouragement — to advance women's rights and economic empowerment.

Unique Carpets

Morocco is known throughout the world for its woven rugs and carpets. Two basic types of carpets are made in Morocco: tribal rugs, also known as Berber rugs, that are made by various Berber tribes in the mountains, and urban rugs, made mostly in Rabat and the town of Mediouna.

For the Berbers, rugs are utilitarian. They are used for warmth, to cover the floors of their tents, and to trade with other tribes for necessities. Berber rugs are small, in part because the weavers use small looms, and in part because the tradition is to cover tent floors with many small, overlapping rugs.

Despite their ordinary purposes, Berber rugs feature intricate geometric patterns made up of diamonds, squares, triangles, and zigzags, and are colored with natural dyes. Each Berber tribe has its own unique designs and patterns; an expert can easily identify which tribe made a rug. Some Berber rugs have lasted for hundreds of years, and even though their colors have faded, the beauty of their craftsmanship remains. Antique Berber rugs

Below: **As the weaving of carpets is a major industry in Morocco, nearly every city and town has at least one store that specializes in the sale of carpets.**

Left: **Morocco has a proud weaving heritage, and many of its rugs and carpets are still handwoven on traditional looms.**

are highly prized by collectors, who are willing to pay huge sums for museum-quality specimens.

Urban rugs are made in small workshops. They are often created for sale to tourists and sold in shops in the souqs or to rug dealers who export them. Their colors are more vivid than the colors of Berber rugs because urban weavers generally use synthetic dyes. Frequently, the rugs have a floral or medallion design in the center, surrounded by borders with intricate geometric designs. Urban rugs can be large enough to cover a room or narrow and long to cover the floor in a hallway.

Both Berber and urban carpets are almost always made by women. Berber women work on small wooden looms, and even though they follow traditional tribal designs and patterns, they do not generally use a pattern or diagram as a guide. As a result, every rug is a unique expression of the weaver's creativity. A Berber woman may be able to weave a small rug in one to two days. Urban weavers follow more specific patterns. A large, room-sized carpet made in an urban workshop may take several months to complete.

Volubilis: Ruins of a Roman City

In A.D. 40, the Roman Empire established the city of Volubilis, one of its farthest outposts, in Morocco. The site chosen had been a Carthaginian settlement since the third century B.C., and it was one of several Carthaginian settlements taken over by Rome after the power of Carthage diminished. The Romans transformed the site into a typical Roman city, complete with temples to the Roman gods, a triumphal arch to honor the emperor, mansions in which Roman officials lived, and a forum, or town center.

From Volubilis, the Romans ruled much of the surrounding countryside, which they used to cultivate wheat and other grains for export throughout the empire. At its height, Volubilis was inhabited not only by Romans, but also by Berbers, Greeks, Jews, and other people from the multiethnic empire. Volubilis remained a Roman city until the fall of the Roman Empire in the third century, and its residents continued to speak Latin and practice

Below: Located near the imperial city of Meknes, Volubilis was a stunning example of Roman architecture dating from the second and third century B.C. Archaeologists suggest that this space, with its massive columns and arches, used to be a courthouse.

Above: **The ancient Roman inscription indicates that this arch in the city of Volubilis was commissioned by Aurelius Antonius.**

Christianity until the arrival of the Arabs in the seventh century. The city was inhabited until the eighteenth century, when it was demolished in order to provide building materials for the construction of the palaces of Moulay Ismail.

Today, the ruins of Volubilis are among the best preserved and most stunning of any ancient Roman city in the world. Most fascinating are the many beautiful mosaics, or decorations made by inlaying colored stones or tiles, that often depicted stories from Roman mythology. Mosaics, which were typically installed on floors, were a principal art form throughout the Roman Empire, and the ones unearthed at Volubilis are among the finest yet discovered. Only about half of the Volubilis site has been excavated, and a team of French and Moroccan archaeologists is working daily to uncover new treasures.

To walk among the ruins of Volubilis is to experience firsthand Roman Morocco and to appreciate the extensive reach of Rome's military power and cultural influence. The huge columns of ancient temples still stand proud; mosaics, some nearly two thousand years old, still sparkle in the bright sun; and grain is still grown in the fields that surround the ancient city.

Western Sahara: A Disputed Land

South of Morocco is a barren, sandy, and sparsely populated territory called Western Sahara. This inhospitable land has been inhabited for centuries by nomadic tribes called Saharawis.

In the late nineteenth century, Western Sahara was colonized by the Spanish, who wanted control of the territory's coastline. Before long, the fiercely independent Saharawis rose in rebellion, launching a guerrilla war and demanding their independence.

Moroccans have always regarded the territory as part of Morocco, basing their claim on traditional pledges of allegiance between Saharawi tribes and Moroccan sultans dating back to the eleventh century. On achieving independence in 1956, Morocco demanded that Spain withdraw from Western Sahara and cede the territory to Morocco. This demand grew even louder in the 1960s, after the discovery of rich deposits of valuable phosphates.

In October 1975, Morocco's king, Hassan II, planned one of the most dramatic events of all time. In what was called "the Green March," over 350,000 Moroccan civilians packed their belongings and began a march to the border of Western Sahara. Not wanting to fire on unarmed civilians, the Spanish withdrew their troops and allowed the "Green Marchers" to enter the territory. The civilians

Below: **Western Sahara is an inhospitable land, but the desert territory has been fiercely disputed since the discovery of phosphates, which are minerals used to make agricultural fertilizer, there.**

were followed closely by the Moroccan army. Morocco won a stunning victory; within months, Spain agreed to give the northern part of Western Sahara to Morocco. They gave the southern part to Mauritania, which, in turn, ceded it to Morocco a few years later.

The struggle over the future of Western Sahara, however, was not over. Many Saharawis refused to accept Moroccan control. They formed a political and military organization called the Polisario that, with the assistance of neighboring Algeria, waged a guerrilla war against Moroccan troops. The two sides declared a cease-fire in 1989, leaving Morocco in control of most of the territory that is protected by the huge wall of sand that Moroccan engineers constructed to keep out Polisario guerrillas.

Western Sahara has increasingly become part of Morocco, even though most nations do not regard it as such. The ongoing struggle between the Moroccan government and the Polisario has been called everything from "Africa's last war of liberation" to "Morocco's struggle for national unity." There are no signs that it will be resolved to the satisfaction of both sides in the near future.

Above: **The Polisario, a military organization made up of Saharawis, and the Moroccan army have fought over control of the Western Sahara for decades. In 1990, the United Nations devised a plan for a referendum that would allow the residents of Western Sahara to vote on whether to become an independent nation. While both Morocco and the Polisario agree to this plan, they have fiercely disagreed over who is eligible to vote.**

RELATIONS WITH NORTH AMERICA

Morocco has had a long and close relationship with North America. In 1777, Morocco became the first country to recognize the United States, which was then fighting its revolution against British rule. During World War II, Morocco was a major staging area for Allied missions in the Mediterranean area, as well as a center of wartime spying. Throughout the Cold War, Morocco was one of the West's closest and most reliable allies and in return received substantial economic aid.

Historically, most Moroccan emigration has been to Europe, but many Moroccans pursue higher education in North America.

Opposite: **A popular tourist destination, Morocco is an attractive location for foreign businesses that rely on tourism, such as the U.S.-based hotel chain, Hyatt.**

The French-speaking Canadian province of Quebec has been a magnet for Moroccan immigrants. Quebec's universities host Moroccan students, and Moroccans seeking jobs and new opportunities are attracted to cities such as Montréal.

An exotic and fascinating country, Morocco is a popular destination for North American tourists. In the 1960s, Morocco was popular with young Americans, especially those who were rebelling against conservative American culture. Today, Morocco attracts many tourists from North America who want to experience the nation's vibrant culture.

Above: **Moroccan kings have always enjoyed a close relationship with the United States. King Mohammed VI met President Bill Clinton in Washington, D.C., soon after assuming the Moroccan throne in 1999.**

Historical Roots of Moroccan–North American Relations

In 1777, Sultan Sidi Mohammed Ben Abdullah granted any merchant ship flying the United States flag the right to dock in Moroccan ports. This gesture made Morocco the first country in the world to recognize the new North American nation.

Treaty of Marrakesh

In 1787, the United States and Morocco signed the formal Treaty of Friendship and Amity, also known as the Treaty of Marrakesh, after the city in which it was negotiated. This treaty was the first such agreement between the United States and any Arab, Muslim, or African nation. In 1821, the Moroccan government gave one of the most beautiful buildings in Tangier to the United States to serve as the United States embassy.

During the U.S. Civil War, Morocco strongly supported the Union and pledged not to offer support to the Confederate forces. In return, at the beginning of the twentieth century, the United States voiced support for Moroccan independence and sovereignty, even as European powers, such as France and Spain, were jockeying for influence and control over Morocco.

Left: Members of the Allied Forces attending the Casablanca Conference pose for a photograph. They are: *(seated, left to right)* U.S. president Franklin D. Roosevelt and British prime minister Winston Churchill; *(standing, left to right)* Admiral E J King, Commander-in-Chief of the U.S. Navy; General George Marshall, U.S. Chief of Staff; Admiral Sir Dudley Pound, Chief of British Naval Staff; General Sir Alan Francis Brooke, Chief of the Imperial General Staff; and Air Chief Marshall Sir Charles Portal.

Allies during the War

In 1942, during World War II, U.S., Canadian, and other allied troops landed in Morocco to prevent an invasion by Germany and to establish a staging area for operations in the Mediterranean. In 1943, U.S. president Franklin D. Roosevelt, British prime minister Winston Churchill, and General Charles DeGaulle, leader of the Free French, met in Casablanca to discuss war strategy. After their meeting, President Roosevelt hosted a dinner in honor of Sultan Mohammed V, at which Roosevelt promised the sultan that the United States would support Morocco's quest for independence. True to Roosevelt's promise, the United States was one of the first nations to recognize Morocco's independence from France in 1956.

Arbitrator of Peace

Under King Hassan II, the U.S.-Moroccan relationship grew even closer. The king was a strong supporter of the West in its struggle against the Soviet Union, and U.S. naval ships were given access to Moroccan ports. Morocco has also traditionally been one of the Arab states most supportive of U.S. efforts to promote the Middle East peace process. King Hassan II played a critical role in bringing about both the Israeli-Egyptian peace treaty in 1979 and the Oslo agreement between Israel and the Palestine Liberation Organization in 1993. During the Gulf War in 1991, Morocco sent troops to bolster U.S. and allied forces against Iraq.

Political Cooperation

Morocco was a principal recipient of U.S. economic and military aid during the Cold War period. The United States has always supported Morocco in its border tensions with neighboring Algeria, which was a Soviet ally during the Cold War, and has encouraged the two nations to reconcile. The U.S. has also tried to mediate the conflict between Morocco and the Polisario in Western Sahara.

Trade and Diplomatic Relations

Although Morocco continues to play a role in U.S. foreign policy, today its importance is more economic than military, with great emphasis placed on promoting U.S.-Moroccan trade and investment. King Mohammed VI has maintained his country's close relationship with the United States, meeting with President Clinton soon after assuming the Moroccan throne. Morocco is also one of the countries in which the U.S. Peace Corps has been most active.

Below: **Morocco's King Mohammed VI meets with U.S. secretary of state Colin Powell at the king's palace in Agadir.**

Relations with Canada

Canada's relationship with Morocco has been based largely on the close ties between Morocco and the French-speaking Canadian province of Quebec. Many Moroccans have emigrated to Quebec for work or study. In fact, government officials in Quebec have actively encouraged Moroccan immigration in order to maintain a favorable balance between French and English speakers in the province. Many Canadian companies based in Quebec also have benefited from the common language by establishing trade and business relationships with Morocco. Over half of the Canadian companies that do business in Morocco are headquartered in Quebec. The Canadian government's official foreign aid agency has provided assistance to Morocco, primarily in the form of Canadian technical expertise.

Above: **Moroccan prime minister Abderrahmane Youssoufi (*right*) accompanies Canadian prime minister Jean Chrétien (*center*) at a guard of honor inspection at Rabat Airport in April 2002.**

Immigration

Most Moroccan immigrants in North America live in Canada, primarily in the province of Quebec. The city of Montreal alone is home to nearly forty thousand Moroccans, including several hundred Moroccan students that are attending colleges and universities. The United States has received fewer immigrants from Morocco, although small Moroccan-American communities can be found in New York, Washington, D.C., Miami, and Los Angeles. In addition, highly trained Moroccans, who are often educated in France, are joining the faculties of U.S. universities in the sciences, Middle Eastern studies, and literature.

Tourism

North American tourists are an important source of income for Morocco. The Moroccan government's tourism agency maintains offices in the United States and Canada to promote travel to Morocco and to work with travel agencies in designing tour packages. Royal Air Maroc, the country's national airline, flies direct to Casablanca from New York and Montreal.

Below: **Morocco's beach resorts offer a wide variety of activities to keep guests occupied. Foreign visitors are often drawn by unusual attractions such as camel rides led by locals dressed in traditional attire.**

Trading Partners

Trade between Morocco and North America is growing, and both the United States and Canada have undertaken programs to encourage greater trade with and investment in Morocco. The U.S. exports around U.S. $750 million worth of goods to Morocco each year and imports around U.S. $250 million worth from the country. Major U.S. exports to Morocco are industrial machinery, aircraft parts, and wheat. U.S. imports from Morocco include seafood, phosphates, textiles, leather goods, and citrus fruits. Canada also imports agricultural goods from Morocco, mainly oranges and olives, and exports to Morocco around U.S. $125 million in wheat and other grains. Both the United States and Canada export more to Morocco than they import, meaning that Morocco has a trade deficit with both North American countries.

Above: **Moroccan exports to the United States include citrus fruits, such as oranges, which are carefully sorted and checked for quality before being packed and shipped.**

Providing Economic Assistance

The United States and Canada have provided millions of dollars in economic assistance to Morocco for decades. This money has been used to improve health care, increase literacy, and modernize agricultural production. In recent years, U.S. and Canadian assistance has focused on providing technical assistance and expertise to the Moroccan private sector. Both the United States and Canada have also set up programs to encourage North American companies and entrepreneurs to invest in Morocco. Currently, the United States is second only to France as the main source of foreign investment in Morocco. The American Chamber of Commerce in Morocco, whose membership includes dozens of U.S. and Moroccan companies, also works to expand business relations between the two countries.

Above: **Morocco has always been open to influences from the West, and drinks such as Coca-Cola are found throughout the country.**

The U.S. Peace Corps in Morocco

In 1961, President John F. Kennedy established the United States Peace Corps, a volunteer organization that sends Americans overseas to spend several years in a developing country, providing assistance and expertise in several important areas. One of the largest and most successful Peace Corps programs has been in Morocco. Since 1963, over four thousand Peace Corps volunteers have served in Morocco, and over one hundred volunteers are currently serving there. Volunteers teach English in rural schools, help build irrigation systems for farms, and advise Moroccan entrepreneurs on how to start and run businesses. Americans who served in the Peace Corps in Morocco have established a private organization called the Friends of Morocco that works to promote stronger U.S.-Moroccan relations, as well as greater understanding and appreciation of Morocco among Americans.

Below: **As part of the Peace Corps program, doctors give children in rural areas free medical check-ups and vaccinations.**

Paul Bowles: An American in Morocco

In the late 1940s, the New York-born composer and writer Paul Bowles traveled to Tangier with his wife. They fell in love with the city and made it their home for the rest of their lives. After Bowles wrote his novel *The Sheltering Sky* in 1949, he became famous. Before long, he and his wife were hosting people who were well known in the worlds of art and literature, turning their Tangier home into a gathering place for artists and writers, and introducing their friends to the allure of Morocco. Bowles wrote several other novels and numerous books on Morocco's culture and aesthetic style. He also translated the works of French and Moroccan authors, published several collections of his photographs of Morocco, and was the subject of a documentary film about his life in Tangier.

In 1990, Italian director Bernardo Bertolucci made a film version of *The Sheltering Sky*, which revived interest in Bowles's work and introduced millions of moviegoers to Morocco. Shortly before his death, Bowles traveled to New York as the guest of honor at a performance of his musical compositions at Lincoln Center. Bowles returned to his adopted home of Tangier soon afterward, where he died in 1999 at the age of eighty-eight.

Left: **American-born writer and composer Paul Bowles sits deep in thought at a park near his home in Tangier. Bowles and his wife fell in love with Morocco when they visited the country and chose to make Morocco their home for nearly fifty years until his death in 1999.**

The Tangier American Legation Museum

In 1821, the Sultan of Morocco gave the United States a building in the medina of Tangier. This building was the first foreign property acquired by the United States. It served as the official U.S. presence in Morocco until 1956, when Morocco achieved independence and all foreign embassies moved to Rabat, the new capital. The United States, however, kept the sultan's gift and used it as an Arabic language school for American diplomats and as a training center for Peace Corps volunteers. In 1976, this building, known in Tangier as the Old American Legation, was declared a U.S. historic landmark — the only building outside of the United States with such a designation — and was converted into the Tangier American Legation Museum.

The building itself dates from the eighteenth century and has been carefully restored. The museum houses an art collection, historical documents related to U.S.-Moroccan relations, and an outdoor courtyard, and has a rooftop with magnificent views of Tangier and the sea. The museum, which is both open to the public and also used for private conferences and receptions, is an enduring reminder of U.S.-Moroccan ties.

Above: Dating back to the eighteenth century, the Tangier American Legation Museum is the only building outside North America that has been declared a U.S. historic landmark.

85

MOROCCO

SPAIN

Strait of Gibraltar
Ceuta (Sp.)
Tangier
16
Tetouan
Asilah
Chaouen
Larache
Jajouka
Al Hoceima
Rif Mountains

ADMINISTRATIVE REGIONS
(Source: Ministry of Communications, Morocco)

Sebou
13
Taounate
Kenitra
Volubilis (Ruins)
Taza
Sale
Moulay Driss
Fez
RABAT
Meknes
14
Ben Slimane
Khemisset
11
Casablanca
Medouna
Middle Atlas Mountains
El-Jadida
10
Boulemane
Settat
Khenifra
12
9
Khouribga
6
Beni Mellal
7
Safi
El Kelaa
des Srarhna
Cascades
d'Ouzoud
Er Rachidia
Marrakesh
Azilal
High Atlas Mountains
5
Essaouira
8
Jebel Toubkal
(13,665 ft / 4,165 m)
Ouarzazate
4
Agadir
Sous
Taroudannt
Zagora
Sous-Massa
National Park
Anti-Atlas Mountains
Tiznit
Tata

#	Region
1	Oued Eddahab-Lagouira
2	Laayoune-Boujdour
3	Guelmim-Es Semara
4	Souss-Massa-Draa
5	Marrakesh-Tensift-El Haouz
6	Doukkala-Abda
7	Tadla-Azilal
8	Meknes-Tafilalet
9	Chaouia-Ouerdigha
10	Casablanca
11	Rabat-Sale-Zemmour-Zaer
12	Fez-Boulemane
13	Gharb-Cherarda-Beni Hssen
14	Taza-El Hoceima-Taounate
15	Oriental
16	Tangier-Tetouan

ATLANTIC OCEAN

Tan-Tan

3

Sahara Desert

Laayoune

Western Sahara

2

MAURITANIA

1

- - - - **International Boundary**
———— **Province Boundary**
■ **Capital**
● **City**
▲ **Highest Point**
◆ **Historical Site**
〜 **River**

E

MEDITERRANEAN
SEA

Melilla (Sp.)
Nador
Oujda
15
Figuig

ALGERIA

N

Above: Dried produce is sold in typical marketplaces in Morocco.

Agadir C3
Al Hoceima D1
Algeria C4-E1
Anti-Atlas Mountains C3
Asilah D1
Atlantic Ocean A4-C1
Azilal D2

Ben Slimane C2
Beni Mellal D2
Boulemane D2

Casablanca C2
Cascades d'Ouzoud D2
Ceuta D1
Chaouen D1

El-Jadida C2
El Kelaa des Srarhna C2
Er Rachidia D2
Essaouira C2

Fez D2
Figuig E2

High Atlas Mountains
   C3-D2

Jajouka D1
Jebel Toubkal C3

Kenitra D2
Khemisset D2
Khenifra D2
Khouribga D2

Layyoune B4

Marrakesh C2
Mauritania A4-E5
Mediouna C2
Mediterranean Sea E1
Meknes D2
Melilla E1
Middle Atlas Mountains D2
Moulay Idriss D2

Nador E1

Ouarzazate D3
Oujda E1
Oum er-Rbia River C2

Portugal C1

Rabat D2
Rif Mountains D1

Safi C2
Sahara Desert C3-D4

Sale D2
Sebou River D1-D2
Settat C2
Sous-Massa National
   Park C3
Spain C1-E1
Strait of Gibraltar D1

Tangier D1
Tan-Tan B3
Taounate D2
Taroudannt C3
Tata C3
Taza D2
Tetouan D1
Tiznit C3

Volubilis D2

Western Sahara A5-C3

Zagora D3

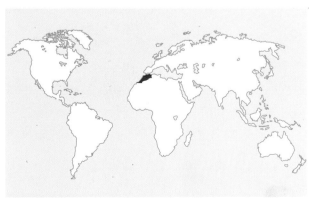

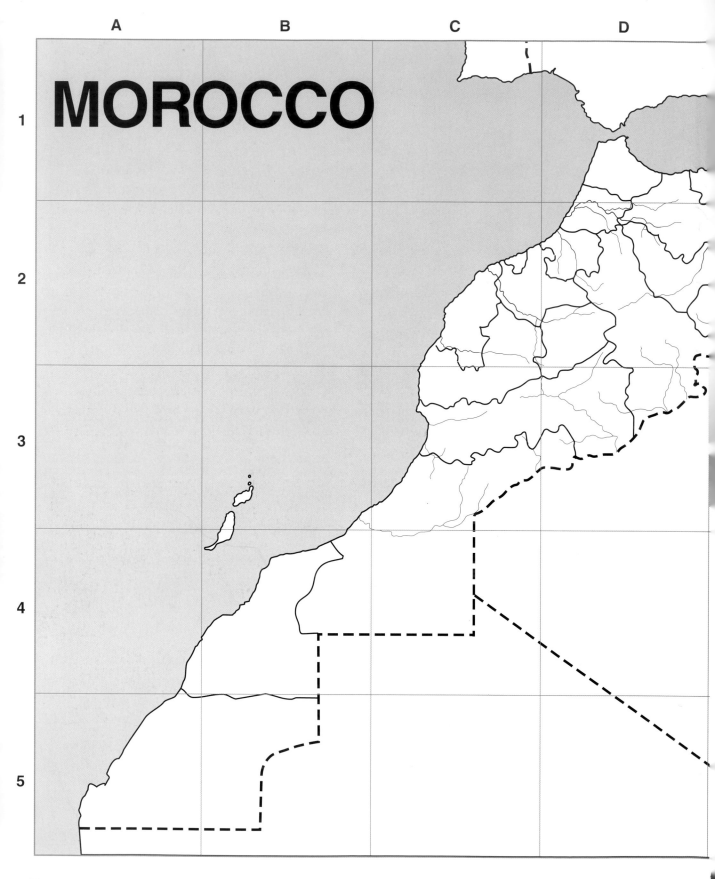

MOROCCO

How Is Your Geography?

Learning to identify the main geographical areas and points of a country can be challenging. Although it may seem difficult at first to memorize the locations and spellings of major cities or the names of mountain ranges, rivers, deserts, lakes, and other prominent physical features, the end result of this effort can be very rewarding. Places you previously did not know existed will suddenly come to life when referred to in world news, whether in newspapers, television reports, other books and reference sources, or on the Internet. This knowledge will make you feel a bit closer to the rest of the world, with its fascinating variety of cultures and physical geography.

Used in a classroom setting, the instructor can make duplicates of this map using a copy machine. (PLEASE DO NOT WRITE IN THIS BOOK!) Students can then fill in any requested information on their individual map copies. Used one-on-one, the student can also make copies of the map on a copy machine and use them as a study tool. The student can practice identifying place names and geographical features on his or her own.

N
↑

Above: **The ruins of the ancient city of Volubilis stand as a reminder of the time when Morocco was part of the Roman Empire.**

Morocco at a Glance

Official Name Kingdom of Morocco

Capital Rabat

Head of State King Mohammed VI

Official Language Arabic

Population 30,645,305 (2001 estimate)

Land Area 172,413 square miles (446,550 square km)

Administrative Regions Casablanca (8 prefectures), Chaouia-Ouerdigha (3 provinces), Doukkala-Abda (2 provinces), Fez-Boulemane (3 prefectures, 2 provinces), Gharb-Cherarda-Beni Hssen (2 provinces), Guelmim-Es Semara (5 provinces), Laayoune-Boujdour (1 prefecture, 1 province), Marrakesh-Tensift-El Haouz (3 prefectures, 4 provinces), Meknes-Tafilalet (2 prefectures, 3 provinces), Oriental (6 provinces), Oued Eddahab-Lagouira (1 province), Rabat-Sale-Zemmour-Zaer (3 prefectures, 1 province), Souss-Massa-Draa (5 provinces, 2 prefectures), Tadla-Azilal (2 provinces), Tangier-Tetouan (3 prefectures, 2 provinces), Taza-El Hoceima-Taounate (3 provinces).

Highest Point Jebel Toubkal 13,665 feet (4,165 m)

Main Religion Islam

Important Leaders Moulay Idriss (?–A.D. 791), Moulay Ismail (1645–1727) King Mohammed V (1909–1961)

Major Holidays New Year's Day (January 1), Independence Manifesto Day (January 11), Labor Day (May 1), National Day (July 30), Reunification Day (August 14), King's and People's Revolution Day (August 20), Anniversary of the Green March (November 6), Independence Day (November 18).

Currency Moroccan Dirhams (10.723 MAD = U.S. $1 as of 2002)

Opposite: **Located in central Morocco, the Cascades d'Ouzoud, the country's most famous waterfall, has a drop of 328 feet (100 m).**

Glossary

Arabic Vocabulary

Allahu akbar (ah-LAH-who-AHK-bar): "God is great."

babouche (bah-BOOSH): traditional leather slippers worn by Moroccans.

darbuka (dah-BOO-kah): a clay drum with a goatskin cover.

Eid al-adha (ead al-AD-hah): feast of the sacrifice, a major Muslim holiday.

Eid al-fitr (ead al-FIT-er): feast of the breaking of the fast that takes place at the end of the month of Ramadan.

harissa (hah-REE-sah): a hot sauce made from peppers, olive oil, and garlic.

iftar (if-TAR): breaking of the fast; the meal held after the sun goes down during the month of Ramadan.

kafta (KAHF-ta): ground lamb, usually served stuffed inside flat bread.

khatib (kha-TEEB): a Muslim cleric who reads the sermon during prayers.

marabout (mar-ah-BOOT): saints or holy men whose tombs are sites of worship.

medina (mah-DEE-nah): the oldest part of a town or city.

mellah (MEL-lah): the traditional Jewish quarter of a Moroccan city.

oud (OUD): a gourd-shaped, stringed instrument.

pastilla (pas-TIL-lah): a pastry stuffed with pigeon meat, eggs, cinnamon, and sugar.

qaidates (kah-EED-ates): the smallest units of government in Morocco.

souq (SOOK): a traditional Moroccan market with many stalls.

tagine (tah-JEEN): a Moroccan stew made with spiced vegetables and meat.

French Vocabulary

baccalauréat (BAH-cah-LOR-ray-ah): the diploma received upon graduation from high school.

English Vocabulary

adherents: followers of a religion or cause.

alms: gifts, usually money, to the poor.

arable: suitable for farming.

arid: dry and parched.

beacon: a tower or any other high structure that serves as a landmark to guide people.

Berbers: people who live in the mountains of north Africa; the earliest inhabitants of Morocco.

bicameral: consisting of two legislative chambers or houses.

black market: the trading or selling of goods outside of the rules and regulations of the law.

calligraphy: artistic and decorative writing.

compulsory: mandatory or obligatory.

constitutional monarchy: a government in which the power of the monarch is limited by a system of written laws.

contraband: goods that are taken into and out of a country illegally.

couscous: a fine grain made from wheat flour; the staple of Moroccan cuisine.

desertification: the expansion of the desert into nearby areas, usually caused by drought and the overuse of agricultural land.

dialects: unique varieties or versions of a particular language.

dynasty: a series of rulers, usually monarchs, from the same family line.

edifices: large and imposing buildings.

empowerment: the giving to a person of the ability to do a particular task.

entombed: placed in a tomb.

entrepreneur: a person who starts a business.

eradicate: remove completely.

extremists: people who hold, and often act on, their beliefs as strongly as possible.

fallow: left uncultivated for one or more growing seasons.

frond: a large and finely divided leaf such as that found in a fern or palm.

hajj: a pilgrimage to the holy city of Mecca that every Muslim is expected to make at least once in his or her life.

homogeneous: composed of similar or identical elements.

hybrid: a mixture or a combination.

illicit: not legally permitted.

imam: a Muslim cleric who leads the recitation of prayers in a mosque.

irrigates: provides water for an otherwise dry area of land.

lineage: the line of descendants of a particular ancestor.

literacy: the ability to read and write.

melds: merges or blends.

minaret: the tower attached to a mosque from which the muezzin calls the people to prayer.

monumental: exceptionally great; usually referring to that which has a historic or enduring significance.

mosaic: colored stones or tiles inlaid and cemented into decorative shapes or pictures on a surface.

muezzin: an announcer, or crier, who calls Muslims to prayer.

paramount: of chief importance.

persecuted: harassed or subjected to cruel treatment or punishment.

Phoenicians: an ancient people, living in what is today Lebanon, who established colonies in the region around the Mediterranean sea.

pilgrimage: a journey to a sacred place of worship.

protectorate: a country which has ceded its governmental authority to another.

razed: demolished.

referendum: the process by which the people of a nation make a decision by voting.

sanctuary: a piece of land where wildlife can live and breed in safety from hunters.

sojourn: a temporary stay.

strait: a narrow passage of water that connects two larger bodies of water.

strongholds: protected places that serve as the centers of operations for groups of people.

subsistence farming: a type of farming in which the food grown meets the needs of the farmer with none left over to sell for cash.

tanneries: places where animal skins are cured and dyed to be made into leather.

utilitarian: having some practical use.

More Books to Read

52 Days by Camel: My Saharan Adventure. Lawrence Raskin (Annick Press)

Morocco. Cultures of the World series. Pat Seward (Benchmark Books)

Morocco. Enchantment of the World series. Ettagale Blauer and Jason Lauré (Children's Press)

Morocco. Major World Nations series. Frances Wilkins (Chelsea House)

Morocco: Past and Present. Guido Barosio, C. T. Milan (Translator) (Michael Publishing Group, Incorporated)

Morocco in Pictures. Visual Geography series. Noel Sheridan (ed.) (Lerner)

North Africa: Morocco. Mira Bartok, Esther Grishman, and Christine Ronan (Goodyear Publishing)

Star of Light. Patricia St. John (Moody Press)

Videos

Eco Challenge: Morocco (Discovery Channel)

Marrakesh and Fez. (Questar)

Morocco: Body and Soul. Seven-film series by Izza Genini. (First Run/Icarus Films)

Royal Families of the World: Japan, Thailand, Morocco, Jordan. (Goldhil Home Media)

Travel the World By Train: Africa - Morocco, Tunisia, Egypt, Kenya, Uganda, South Africa (Pioneer, LDCA)

Web Sites

www.arab.net/morocco/morocco_contents.html

www.mincom.gov.ma

www.usembassy-morocco.org.ma/

Due to the dynamic nature of the Internet, some web sites stay current longer than others. To find additional web sites, use a reliable search engine with one or more of the following keywords to help you locate information about Morocco. Keywords: *Berbers, Casablanca, Fez, Green March, Hassan II Mosque, Rabat, Treaty of Marrakesh, Volubilis.*

Index

Allahu akbar 27
Alaouite 13, 15, 48, 53
Algeria 6, 13, 15, 47, 73, 78
Almohad 12, 46, 53
Almoravid 12, 46, 52
agriculture 18, 20
animals 9, 30, 33
Anti-Atlas Mountains 7, 28
Arabic 5, 25, 28, 29, 30, 47
Arabs 12, 20, 31, 52, 71
architecture 30, 43, 70
Asilah 33
Atlantic Ocean 6, 7

babouche 63
Baghdad 15
baccalauréat 25
Belgium 18
Berbers 3, 5, 10, 12, 15, 20,
    27, 28, 29, 31, 32, 39, 43,
    44, 46, 47, 52, 68, 70
bicameral legislature 16
birds 9
black market 21
Bowles, Paul 84
bread 40
Byzantines 11

calligraphy 30
camels 5
Canada 19, 35, 79, 80, 81, 82
carpets 31, 32, 33, 47, 62,
    63, 68, 69
Carthage 10, 11, 70
Casablanca 6, 19, 20, 30, 36,
    54, 55, 80
cellular phones 19
Ceuta 12
Chamber of Counselors
    16, 17
Chamber of Representatives
    16, 17

children 22, 23, 24, 25, 35, 41,
    43, 47, 66, 67
Churchill, Winston 76, 77
citrus fruits 18, 81
Commander of the Faithful
    17, 48
constitutional monarchy 5,
    14, 16
cork oak 9
couscous 40

darbukas 31
dates 18
Delacroix, Ferdinand Victor
    Eugene 44
deserts 5, 7, 44, 60
dessert 41
dialects 28, 47

economy 16, 18, 19, 21
education 21, 24, 25, 49, 66
Egypt 15
Eid al-Adha 38
Eid al-Fitr 38
Europe 5, 6, 12, 13, 19, 21, 35,
    43, 44, 56, 57, 60
European Union 19

family 13, 17, 22, 23, 34, 35,
    38, 48, 49, 55, 59, 66, 67
festivals 33, 34, 38, 39, 61
Fez 6, 7, 12, 25, 32, 33, 49,
    52, 53, 56, 57, 61
fishing 6, 18
food 18, 40, 41, 50, 65
France 13, 17, 18, 29, 44, 49,
    53, 57, 76, 77, 80, 82
French 5, 13, 15, 25, 28, 29,
    41, 44, 47, 48, 51, 53, 54,
    57, 60, 71, 75, 77, 79, 84

Germany 13, 36, 57, 77

Gibraltar, Strait of 6, 9
golf 36
government 14, 16, 17,
    18, 21, 24, 27, 48, 49,
    60, 61, 64, 65, 66, 67,
    73, 76, 79
Green March 72
Guerrouj, Hicham al- 37

hajj 26
Hand of Fatima 32
handicrafts 18, 32
harissa 40
Hassan II 14, 17, 36, 48, 49,
    54, 55, 57, 67, 72, 77
Hassan II Mosque 30, 54
health care 21, 82
Hebrew 26
High Atlas Mountains
    7, 28
holidays 22, 34, 38, 39, 40

Idriss, Moulay 12, 15, 27,
    39, 53
Idriss II 52
Idrissid 12
iftar 38
imams 27
Imilchil 39
imperial cities 6, 52, 53
independence 5, 11, 13, 14,
    21, 24, 29, 57, 66, 72, 76,
    77, 85
Internet 19, 23
Islam 5, 12, 26, 27, 30, 33,
    43, 46, 48, 54, 55, 56
Islamic law 17, 23, 49

Israel 56, 57, 77
Jajouka 31
Jebel Toubkal 7
jewelry 5, 32, 47, 65

Jews 5, 20, 26, 27, 32, 43, 56, 57, 70

kafta 41
Kennedy, John F. 83
khatibs 27
Khourigba 18
Krim, Abd el- 15

language 10, 25, 28, 29, 31, 46
leather 18, 32, 47, 62, 63, 81
Libya 47
literacy 24, 66, 82
literature 25, 28, 29
Louis XIV 15, 53

marabout 27
Marathon of the Sands 36, 50, 51
Marinid 12
Marrakesh 6, 8, 24, 26, 30, 52, 53
Matisse, Henri 45
Mauritania 6, 73
Mecca 26, 55
medinas 52, 62
Mediterranean Sea 6, 9, 12
Meknes 6, 11, 15, 52, 53, 70
Melilla 12
mellahs 56
Mediouna 58
Mernissi, Fatima 29
Middle Atlas Mountains 7, 28, 39, 53
minarets 30, 54, 55
mint tea 41, 59, 63
Mohammed (prophet) 15, 16, 17, 26, 32, 39, 48
Mohammed V (Mohammed Ben Youssef) 13, 14, 15, 49, 57, 77
Mohammed VI 14, 49, 75, 78
mosaics 55, 71

mosques 26, 27, 30, 53
Moulay Idriss (town) 15
Moutawakil, Namal al- 37
muezzins 27, 30
museums 32, 33, 85
music 31, 35, 39, 43
Muslims 5, 12, 15, 20, 26, 27, 28, 38, 52, 55, 56

oases 9
Olympic Games 37
Oum er-Rbia 7
ouds 31

Palestine Liberation Organization 57, 77
parliament 14, 16, 67
pastilla 40
Peace Corps 78, 83, 85
Phoenicians 10
phosphates 18, 72, 81
pilgrimages 15
plants 9
Polisario 73, 78
political parties 17
population growth 18, 21, 24, 65
ports 6, 11, 19, 76, 77
Portugal 13
poverty 18, 21, 55
Powell, Colin 78
prayer 27, 38, 39
protectorate 13, 48

Quebec 75, 79, 80
Qur'an 26, 27, 28, 30, 49, 66

Rabat 6, 16, 17, 33, 36, 52, 53, 66, 68, 79, 85
Ramadan 26, 38
religion 12, 25, 26, 27, 46, 56
Rif Mountains 7, 12, 15, 28, 31
Roman Empire 11, 70, 71

Romans 11, 56, 70
Rome 43, 70
Roosevelt, Franklin D. 76, 77

Sahara Desert 7, 8, 11, 20, 36, 50, 64
Saharawis 20, 21, 72, 73
Seal of Solomon 5
Sebou 7
soccer 23, 35, 36
souqs 32, 52, 53, 58, 62, 63, 69
Spain 11, 12, 13, 17, 18, 20, 26, 31, 40, 43, 52, 56, 72, 73, 76
spices 40, 62, 63
sports 23, 36, 51
Strait of Gibraltar 6, 9

tagine 40
Tangier 6, 10, 15, 33, 44, 76, 84, 85
temperatures 8, 50, 51
textiles 18, 62, 81
Tiffany, Louis Comfort 44
tourism 18, 36, 51, 75, 80
Tunisia 10, 47

unemployment 18
United Nations 73
United States 19, 35, 60, 75, 76, 77, 78, 80, 81, 82, 85
universities 25, 75, 80

Vandals 11
Versailles 15, 53
Volubilis 11, 15, 70, 71

Washington, D.C. 57, 75, 80
weddings 26, 34, 38
Western Sahara 6, 7, 17, 20, 21, 64, 72, 73, 78
World Cup 36
World War II 13, 57, 60, 75, 77